Also by Judith C. Tingley

*Genderflex: Men and Women Speaking
Each Other's Language*

*Say What You Mean, Get What You Want: A Businessperson's
Guide to Direct Communication*

GenderSell
How to Sell to the Opposite Sex

Judith C. Tingley, Ph.D., and Lee E. Robert

Simon & Schuster

SIMON & SCHUSTER
Rockefeller Center
1230 Avenue of the Americas
New York, NY 10020

SIMON & SCHUSTER and colophon are registered trademarks
of Simon & Schuster Inc.

Designed by DEIRDRE C. AMTHOR

Manufactured in the United States of America

10 9 8 7 6 5 4 3 2 1

Library of Congress Cataloging-in-Publication Data
Tingley, Judith C.
GenderSell: how to sell to the opposite sex / Judith C. Tingley,
Lee E. Robert.
      p   cm.
Includes bibliographical references and index.
    1. Selling.   2. Sex differences (Psychology)
3. Selling—Psychological aspects.   4. Consumer behavior
5. Women consumers.   6. Male consumers.   I. Robert, Lee E.
                    II. Title.
    HF5438.25.T56   1999   98-42000
    658.85—dc21   CIP
              ISBN 0-684-84385-4

GenderSell is a registered trademark of Judith Tingley.

Contents

Introduction:
It's Time to Raise the Bar
for Sales Skills

Selling is an art. Done well, it may be one of the most complex and satisfying forms of mutual influence that takes place in the world of business. Done poorly, it can be a manipulative, gamey, dispiriting contest between apparent adversaries. In the late twentieth century, sales books and training have emphasized building relationships, solving problems, and consultation as desired approaches. This more educational mode advances the professionalism of sales and caters to the increasing demands of consumers for service, information, and courtesy.

The sales professionals of the next century, however, need to further refine and upgrade their skills by selling one-to-one. What does that mean? It means tailoring the sales and service approach to the uniqueness of each individual so that the customer experiences a custom fit. It means understanding the contribution that specific factors such as gender have on customers' needs for information and their wants for a comfortable sales process.

Times have changed. The old ways no longer work. Salespeople who don't adapt to an increasingly diverse, complex, and worldly population, and who continue to "prey" on customers in traditional game-playing fashion, may find themselves the victims of tomorrow.

Gendersell is an advanced, timely, and forward-looking approach to the sales process. The coined verb denotes "using communication techniques typical of the other gender in order to increase potential for influence in sales situations."

Sales is an influence situation. As an interpersonal process, it is subject to the same psychosocial principles that apply to all kinds of influence circumstances. People are more apt to like, be comfortable with, and be influenced by people they see as similar to themselves. The greater the perceived similarity—at least along lines that have relevance to the sale—the greater the potential influence. For example, if a customer is a Macintosh user who is buying software, she'll be more readily influenced by a salesperson who is also a Mac user than one who is a PC person. If she is buying a refrigerator, the Mac similarity will count for less.

Salespeople for years have used the approach of observing their customer's surroundings and commenting on the family picture, the mounted boar head, the golf trophies, or framed awards. Often they have attempted to tie in to some sameness. "I'm a golfer, too," or "My daughters are probably just about the same age as yours," recognizing the power of similarities.

The Gendersell approach takes the influence process to a higher level. Certainly we encourage you as a salesperson—whether you're selling products or services, one-to-one or business-to-business; whether you're selling wholesale or retail; whether you're selling financial services, flowers, or concepts—to comment on apparent similarities between you and your customer. However, we recommend even more strongly that you think and communicate in a way similar to them, to sell to them as they want to be sold to, to understand them more thoroughly than ever before, to be the most flexible, adaptable, insightful salesperson your customers have ever met—particularly with the customers who are very different from you: those of the opposite sex.

Along with other commentators on male-female differences and similarities, we believe that gender is the biggest difference found across ethnicities, nationalities, and religions. Bridging the gap between the male salesperson and the female customer, or vice versa, takes more thought, more work, and more adaptation than most transactions.

Certainly all men and all women are not the same. There are

similarities between the genders as well as differences. As we write about men, in general, and women, in general, some readers may find that not all of our observations apply to them. They may feel stereotyped when we say that women care more about relationships than men or that men care more about money than women. We're speaking in generalities (based on a vast amount of research), referring to most men and women under various circumstances, rather than the stereotype of all men and women at all times. We focus on the differences between men and women in this book because the differences, not the similarities, are often the obstacles to success.

Our premise is that salespeople who are attuned to the increasing diversity in markets, who are adept at tailoring their approach to the differences in customers, and who are skilled in delivering messages unique to each customer will attain the most success now and in the next century.

Lee Robert is a director of sales and marketing at Corporate Education and Consulting. I (Judy) am a consultant on gender and communication in the workplace. While we pursued our speaking engagements and training workshops, working with men and women in sales in a variety of different fields, we found that sales professionals often don't know how to customize their approach to the uniqueness (gender or otherwise) of their clients. Many have learned a step-by-step process that their company teaches, and they stick with it most of the time with most of the customers; it may even be the same process they learned years ago as a new salesperson. Or they may have their own preference for sales style, based on their experience, and they follow that style most of the time with most of their customers.

We also found, however, that many of our audience members wanted information specifically about selling to the opposite sex, particularly in industries that were nontraditional for one sex or the other: selling trucks or golf club memberships to women or household appliances and cooking classes to men.

We also learned in our conversations with sales professionals that no one had experienced sales training that focused on selling to the opposite sex. Most of the people we interviewed said they wanted specifics about communication and influence techniques tailored to their opposite gender. Questions ranged from "Is it okay to be slightly flirtatious in a sales situation with a man if that clearly works to keep his attention?" to "I can't seem to find that fine line between being too firm and focused when I'm selling to women and being friendly and accessible. This is business, after all, not a social relationship." Other concerns were also expressed: "I can't tell if the man is just testing me or if he's really serious about the sale. I don't know when to stop wasting my time." Or "I often get frustrated with how slowly women make decisions. Then I get pushy, but that never works and I don't know what else to do."

We found that there was little written about the topic of selling and marketing differently to the opposite sex. An amazing number of books, new and old, were written by men for men in sales, about selling to male customers. Few were written by women or even mentioned gender or women. We concluded that most of what has been taught in sales was based on men selling to men and excluded women selling to men, men selling to women, and women selling to women.

To add to the data on gender differences and sales techniques, we developed the Sales Preference Survey. Distributed to more than six hundred consumers, it proved that men and women see male and female sales professionals very differently in terms of their assets and their liabilities. They see differing qualities and characteristics in male and female sales professionals as important. For example, honesty was more frequently stressed as important for men, while friendliness was mentioned for women.

Another significant finding was that respondents saw products as gendered. Consumers seemed to prefer buying a specifically gendered product from a specifically gendered salesperson. For example, jewelry was seen as female and financial services as male; houses as female but office buildings as male. Both men and women stated a preference for buying jewelry from women and financial services from men because they saw salespeople as more knowledgeable about a product that was similar to themselves in gender.

Women and men both stated a preference for working with the same-sex salesperson, although with some exceptions. We think that preference has less to do with the actual sex of the salesperson than it does with the perceived similarity or difference in the communication process used. Men and women as consumers tend to prefer their own sex as salespeople because they believe their own gender speaks the same language. But if female sales professionals can learn more "male talk" and males can learn more "female talk" using Gendersell techniques, the perception that one gender is preferable for selling a specific product or service will probably disappear.

What the sales professional can also learn from the Gendersell approach is how to be perceived as more knowledgeable about an "opposite sex" product or service—such as a woman selling cars or a man selling art. You can learn how men and women think, communicate, and act when shopping and buying, and use that information to increase your effectiveness by altering the perceptions of your opposite-sex customer.

Some companies, entrepreneurs, and sales professionals have already seen the need for viewing the gender of the consumer as a critical factor in designing an adaptive approach to marketing, advertising, and selling. BMW figured out several years ago that it needed to sell and market differently if it wanted to sell more cars to women. To this end they designed a full-scale marketing opportunity approach, focused on promoting, advertising, and selling more adaptively. Their efforts resulted in a 7 percent increase in female clients plus an increase in the customer satisfaction level of men as well as women.

About Women, Inc., a Boston, Massachusetts, company founded by Jann Leeming, recognized the need for a different approach to selling and marketing to women. She founded a newsletter, *About Women and Marketing,* which is now the premier source of information about female-male similarities and differences as consumers.

MacDonald Communications, the publisher of *Working Woman, Working Mother,* and *Ms.* magazine, sponsored the first annual Marketing to Women Congress in 1997. They emphasized marketing and advertising differently to men and women as consumers of automobiles, health care, and financial services, and as online customers. Representatives from major corporations of various industries participated in this public forum about the importance of adapting to customer gender differences now and into the next century.

The Martz Agency is an advertising and public relations firm based in Phoenix, Arizona, that has begun to specialize in gender-specific advertising. According to their research, men and women respond differently to TV, print, and radio, as well as to images, color, words, and advertising style. First, they determine statistically whether the target market is mostly male, mostly female, or mixed. They then design their campaign to fit the gender of the customer most likely to purchase the product advertised, whether it is golf clubs or cars, houses or food, computers or cigars. Martz is on the leading edge of this type of advertising but will undoubtedly be quickly joined by other agencies.

Looking at success from another angle, Deloitte Consulting is concentrating on women doing a better job of selling to men. Their Initiative for the Retention and Advancement of Women, formally begun in 1993, has been remarkably successful in increasing the number of women recruited into the firm. Now, however, those in the highest management positions have recognized a potential barrier to these women's promotion: They have more trouble than men of equivalent backgrounds in building the kind of professional relationships with male clients that lead to further business. The company is therefore offering training that will give them more effective influencing techniques with the opposite sex.

IBM is a company that has recognized the need to market and

sell differently to women. They developed a task force to study the specific needs of women business owners and found that a prime commonality was their desire for loyalty, nurturing, and caring relationships from their vendors. IBM used that data to design a marketing approach that focused on contacting women through business associations and to develop a sales approach that focused on the one-to-one connection of women to women. Their approach was so successful nationally that they are now expanding it internationally under the direction of Cherie Piebes, the Global Market Director for Women Entrepreneurs.

No amount of marketing and advertising will work, however, if the customer gets hit over the head with a "one size fits all" sales approach. The sales process has to be more targeted and customized than that marketing and advertising approach. It has to be one-to-one sales aimed specifically, but not exclusively, at the gender of the customer. The Gendersell techniques are creating a top echelon of professional salespeople who are leading the charge into the twenty-first century by selling successfully to the opposite sex.

Chapter 1
Customizing for Consumer Gender

Consumers in the United States are more demanding, knowledgeable, worldly, and difficult to please than ever. People of all ages, of both genders, of different races, ethnicity, and religions, in nontraditional occupations and roles are buying products and services they have never bought before. There are hundreds of emerging trends among and between customers that will challenge the sales professional of the future as never before.

The tendency of men and women to change, merge, and separate as consumers is the number one trend, ripe for the attention of smart sales professionals. Changing demographics in the United States related to women and men, their occupations and careers and their roles and responsibilities at home and at work, have dramatically altered the customer base for a broad variety of products and services. Many buyers of traditionally "male" products in the U.S. marketplace are now women, while more and more men are buying what were once considered "female" products and services.

For example, male engineers and computer nerds aren't the only people buying modems and laptops. Housewives, househusbands, interior designers, architects, retail store owners, and home-based business owners are all getting in line and online. Men are buying household appliances, groceries, and their own clothes. They are purchasing plastic surgery, facials, and manicures. They're buying single-parent houses and the Oriental rugs and artwork to go with them. Meanwhile, women are buying office buildings, stocks, and cigars. They are playing golf and joining country clubs. They are purchasing business travel and disability insurance.

A large number of business equipment customers are now at home instead of in high-rises—either telecommuting or conducting home-based businesses. These are people who need fax machines, phones, modems, and computers. (Will the old Fuller Brush salesperson be replaced by the door-to-door business equipment sales pro?) Many of these home-based businesses are female-owned, and their main contact with the world of commerce is through their computer.

Small and large businesses are trying to catch up or stay ahead of all the changes in the marketplace: changes in products, in services, in target markets, and in customers. A print shop owner was stunned to see his customer base move from 100 percent male purchasers to more than 80 percent female purchasers in less than three years. He was not prepared for this change and didn't have the needed sales skills. He is still trying to adapt.

In contrast, BMW leaped ahead of its competitors by taking advantage of changing trends. The market for BMWs is no longer white men between thirty-five and fifty. It is women as well, both young and old. This change was anticipated and orchestrated. BMW was ready for the leap in the percentage of female buyers because it foresaw the changes in male and female roles, interests, and lifestyles.

A new monthly publication, *Connect Time,* is distributed through local newspapers. The news magazine format which is focused on people, is colorful, warm, and friendly. The stated goal is to put a human face on technology. In our opinion, the magazine is aimed at the female population of recreational computer users, but its editor says the target market is people intimidated by the Internet who would like a more comfortable relationship with it. The editor said that more men suffer from Internet phobia than women. Talk about a niche market!

Gender—the Big Difference
Between Customers

All these dramatic changes point strongly to the need for distinct approaches to marketing, advertising, and selling to the two genders. We all know that men and women are different—in the way we look and think, in the way we talk and behave, in the way we use computers and grills, in our TV preferences, in our favorite vacation spots, and even in our food choices. We can usually laugh about some of our most common differences even if they also seem to fit a stereotype. For example, many men refuse to ask for directions; women often cry at the drop of a hat.

Because men and women are different as shoppers and buyers, and because they are different types of communicators, they want to be treated differently by salespeople. One size never fits all, nor does one sales approach work equally well with men and women. For example, I (Judy) see tremendous differences in the way my husband and I shop. Although neither of us necessarily epitomizes the average man and woman, our specific gender differences are probably representative of the majority in certain aspects of the purchasing process.

For example, Mike enjoys buying a car in one day. He puts aside the entire afternoon to negotiate the deal. He has done all the research ahead of time, without benefit of any relationship with a salesperson or any test drive in the desired model. He generally knows what he wants and goes to buy it. He enjoys the gamesmanship of the bargaining process. It is a competitive challenge to negotiate with the salesperson and to get a great deal. He is focused on the task at hand and enjoys the traditional haggling process.

In contrast, I see the car-buying process as potentially a month-long adventure. I like to look at all kinds of cars, to drive a variety of models, to think and talk about and savor the shopping, culminating in a final decision after lengthy conversations with friends and family.

We usually approach the *whole process* of buying differently, regardless of what product or service we are purchasing. Some of these differences may have to do with personality and experience, but in most cases they stem from the fact that he's a man and I'm a woman.

Other couples often notice gender differences when shopping for clothes. Occasionally Patti's husband, Pete, will go with her to the mall. He goes only when he thinks the trip will be short and Patti wants his opinion on a particular special item: a suit, dress, or bathing suit, perhaps. Pete heads straight for the rack where Patti's size is, pulls out the item in the color she says she wants, and proclaims, "Here it is. This is just what you wanted, and I like it. Try it on." "Let's go" is the unspoken follow-up.

Inevitably, even if the dress or suit fits perfectly and is in the right price range, Patti wants to look around a little more, try on a few more things, and check out a couple more stores. Pete consistently feels confused and duped. He thought they came to buy something, not to look around. Patti intends to buy something, but not quite so quickly or easily.

This stream of gender difference is endless—not for each of us or all of us or all the time, but for many of us most of the time, in a broad variety of settings and contexts. All these differences in thinking, perception, and behavior translate into specific differences in men and women as consumers and as your customers.

About Women and Marketing details research about gender-different responses to products, services, and advertising. Knowing this type of information can help sales professionals understand and enhance their approach to the opposite sex. For the most part the following examples hold true:

- Women use computers. Men love them. Women think of them as similar to an appliance. Men think of them as similar to a friend.
- When planning a wedding, men are mostly interested in the

food and drink; women, in the church, the music, the dresses, and rings.

• Women and men both like beer, but women's tastes in beer are often different from men. They also object to the total male focus in beer advertising.

• Men may take three months to pick out a new car. But unlike women, who get the rap for being slow decision-makers when shopping for cars, men spend that three months reading and researching on their own, often not even visiting a dealership until they have decided exactly what they want and what they are going to pay.

• Men don't like shopping for holiday gifts. They see it as a task to be done as quickly and efficiently as possible. They want quick solutions. Women generally enjoy shopping more, are better bargain hunters, and take more time to look for and pick out what they think is just the right gift.

• Men use senior discounts to a higher degree than women.

• Women are generally more concerned with health care in general, and choosing the right physician, in particular, than are men.

• All other things being equal, women are more likely to buy a product from a company that clearly demonstrates a corporate conscience than one that doesn't. Anita Roddick's Body Shop is a good example (although there has been some recent doubt about just how "green" she really is). She does no animal testing of products and uses primarily renewable natural materials. She subsidizes day care and runs child development centers for her employees in the United Kingdom. Her products may or may not be any better than those of comparable companies, but her global community outlook and her caretaking mentality appeal to her female customers.

• Women are interested in learning golfspeak even before they learn to play golf so they can listen and talk intelligently with male colleagues about their golf game.

- In making buying decisions about computers, women rely more heavily on service, price, and the vendor's reputation and experience than men do.
- Men are more interested in antibacterial agents in soap. Women are more interested in moisturizing and fragrance. As men are becoming more concerned about skin care, they are more interested in the moisturizers but still don't go for floral smells, light or not. A new unisex soap is in the works.
- Women are playing and watching sports in much greater numbers than ever before.

Clearly, understanding the gender differences in focus, interests, and behavior in your industry or relevant to your specific product can be a major contribution to success in closing the deal.

Gender—a Big Difference Between Sales Professionals

If men and women are different as customers, then they are certainly also different as salespeople. As part of the hands-on research for *Gendersell,* I (Judy) went shopping for a car. I knew that the communication and relationship skills of the salesperson would be even more important in my final decision than the specific car I was buying. I could connect psychologically with the people. I wouldn't connect with the car, at least not with the same intensity.

What I had hoped would be an enjoyable experience turned into the all-too-familiar automotive odyssey—a circus of bungling gamesmanship. But I observed some definite gender differences in the way salespeople behave and communicate.

I chose two different makes and two different models to investigate, two different dealerships, and two different salespeople with whom to work. Both Joe and Dorothy behaved in somewhat expected and stereotypic sex-role ways. Dorothy talked too much about her personal life and didn't talk enough about the car. She gave the wrong prices and was overly apologetic. She was clearly sincere but not a strong influencer or an assertive seller. Joe asked and talked too little about my needs and wants, listened too little to what I said, and pushed too much to sell what he had instead of what I wanted. He seemed to be playing a familiar, scripted game and was annoyed because I didn't know or didn't play by the rules.

In this story, Joe's sales techniques don't necessarily represent those of all male salespeople, just as Dorothy's don't reflect those of all female salespeople. Still, they each behaved in ways that are generally characteristic of their particular gender. Dorothy's conversation about herself and the personal aspects of her current life situation are communication approaches found more commonly in women than in men. In general, women are less direct in their communication and prefer and often produce a more soft sell approach to sales.

Joe exhibits characteristics of many men, both in and out of sales. He is playing by certain rules that he expects the customer to play by as well. He is not as interested in the relationship as he is in the deal. His focus is on playing the selling game according to the prescribed ritual, not on establishing a long-term relationship with the consumer as a present and future customer. He is thinking about the here and now, and making it happen. Dorothy is thinking about the longer term relationship.

Are there salesmen who are more relationship oriented than saleswomen are? Are there saleswomen who are very direct and more interested than Dorothy in talking about their product? Of course there are. But our survey research shows that customers perceive the same general gender differences in salespeople that I noticed while working with Joe and Dorothy.

Customers want it all, from both male and female sales professionals. They want caring. They want depth and breadth of knowledge. They want to be understood. They want a friendly, genuinely interested approach. They want intelligence and good looks. They want assertiveness but not aggressiveness. They want confidence but not cockiness. They want expertise and experience with the product or service.

Women customers may want a different ratio of friendliness to product knowledge than their male counterparts; male customers may care more about the product than they do about the salesperson's approach. For the learning salesperson, improving your ability to read customers and influence or persuade them based on their gender is an advanced skill that will ultimately ensure more and better sales to a particularly diverse customer base.

What Gender Is Your Product or Service?

If the gender of the sales professional interacting with the gender of the customer isn't enough to add complexity to the already intricate sales situation, there are theorists who assert that products have a clear gender, too. Pamela Alreck's article in the *Journal of Product and Brand Management* points out that there are basic masculine and feminine products: those associated with use by one sex or the other (for example, panty hose, after-shave lotion, makeup, and jockstraps). But, she notes, many products purchased and used by both sexes are imbued with a masculine or feminine image in design, advertising, promotion, and distribution. For example, sporting goods, barbecues, garden tools, movies, books, and cars can be promoted as gendered products and made to fit either the masculine or feminine role.

A barbecue could be positioned as "a giant power king of a barbecue" for the guy who likes to grill a half side of venison, or it can be positioned as a big but lightweight barbecue that can cook a whole meal at a time. Alreck cautions that women will accept masculine-gendered brands, but men almost totally reject feminine-gendered brands. (For example, women will buy male-gendered bikes, but almost all men would reject female-gendered bikes.)

While men have traditionally been averse to feminine-gendered brands or items, only recently have women begun to reject male-gendered items. They are demanding equipment, sports clothing, and even business and sports magazines that are constructed as well as gendered specifically for women. One *Inc.* magazine reader commented that she wished articles were constructed so that readers didn't have to be wearing a jock strap to understand them.

While the idea that products and services are in fact gendered may be a new concept to you, it is common knowledge to the consumers responding to the Sales Preference Survey. These same consumers/respondents also seemed to think that most of the time a salesperson who is of the same gender as his or her product or service sells it the best.

If a woman in sales can use a "male" approach to sell a male product and if a man in sales can use a "female" approach to sell a female product, they will both boost their success rate. And this ability is the foundation of becoming a Gendersell expert.

Chapter 2
Adapting to Difference

Companies such as Domino's Pizza need to be ever flexible in creating appropriate toppings for new global markets, from mayonnaise potato pizza in Tokyo and pickled ginger pizza in India to reindeer-sausage pizza in Iceland. How did Domino's come up with these unusual ideas? The same way you as salespeople are going to come up with different approaches to your opposite-sex customers—through research, creativity, and flexibility. For salespeople, adaptability is pivotal in obtaining a bigger share of the market.

What more do you need to know about male-female similarities and differences in order to be a superstar Genderseller? Lots. The more you know and understand about the opposite gender, the less you are limited by assumptions. Open your mind to the probability that women are going to be the primary purchasers online, even though they've been slower than men getting on the Internet, because shopping by computer will save them time. Recognize that men are beginning to appreciate quality and the comforts of life. Be aware that when choosing a car, women have criteria other than color and safety; image and class are both becoming more important. Accept that the ads which appeal to men often don't elicit a positive response from women. Notice that men and women are continuing to expand the boundaries of acceptable interests and styles within their typical gender roles.

Sales professionals, perhaps even more than people in other

occupations, need to constantly conduct an attitude assessment to make sure they have maintained an open-minded, curious, non-judgmental approach to people and knowledge. The more receptive you are to information that contradicts what you have always believed or what you have experienced in the past, the more creative and flexible you can become in your day-to-day approach. And you will have more fun in addition to making more sales.

Mike, a salesman we interviewed, admitted that he really isn't good at selling cars to women because he just can't treat them with respect. Why? Because he doesn't respect them as drivers. His specific complaint was that he disliked the habit of some women to apply makeup while driving, a practice he found stupid as well as unsafe.

Mike may be absolutely right, but to give up potential sales to at least half of his customer base because of a personal prejudice doesn't make sense. If he could adopt a more open-minded attitude, he'd move a long way toward greater success with female customers.

Similarly, women in sales who won't deal with men because they fear that they will come across as pushy are also missing out on potential sales. Although many men may not particularly like aggressiveness in either male or female sales professionals, they still buy from pushy men—and they'll probably buy from pushy women, too. In addition, men may have a considerably higher threshold than women for translating "enterprising" into "overaggressive." Opening your mind to different ways of thinking about yourself, your customer, the way you interact, and the gender dynamics at work is a good way to start selling to the opposite sex more effectively.

Where Do Male-Female Differences Come From?

There is no doubt about the enormous differences between men and women, although there may be dispute about where they originate. The nature/nurture controversy has surged and receded over the years. Historically, psychological theory has attributed gender differences to how we are raised and what we are taught about becoming boys and men and girls and women. Although the media is full of articles about changing roles for men and women in contemporary society, old stereotypes still strongly affect how men and women *believe* they should think, act, and be, as well as what products and services they should, can, and will buy.

Pamela Alreck's article in the *Journal of Product and Brand Management* also pointed out that clear expectations about contemporary sex roles still exist: masculine strength, feminine gentleness, male freedom, and female attachment. Even today, men are expected to be tough-minded, decisive, and independent. Men are supposed to be competitive, powerful, and cool. A man should never show too much emotion. He must also be a breadwinner— the primary source of income for his family. A woman is expected to always behave like a lady, a role with many connotations concerning actions, communication, and dress. Women are expected to be nurturing, warm, and caring, putting home and family above all other interests. Yet the woman of the 90s also wants to be viewed as strong, independent, and intelligent.

Even with today's changing mores, many people still require adherence to our ingrained rules about sex roles. If a man is to be pictured or portrayed in the media as crying, the tears can only be brief and infrequent. The circumstances must be extreme. The small window of sex-role overlap in advertising may allow a woman to be depicted as a construction worker, for example, but preferably one who is attractive and carefully made up. Violation of these rules, particularly in attempting to "gender" a product or service, is dangerous. For example, attempting to focus diaper sales on the male market by depicting men as househusbands and women as the primary breadwinners would probably not make a hit. In contrast, depicting a husky, sweaty woman in overalls and a baseball cap, pushing and promoting a lawnmower on TV, won't persuade most female viewers.

The power of socialization as a predictor of shopping and buying behavior of men and women can't be underestimated. Nevertheless, not recognizing the dramatic shift from *Leave It to Beaver* days can also destroy a sale.

Felipe, a thirty-something stockbroker friend who considers himself enlightened about gender roles in contemporary society, found out just how hard it is to sell to a couple. In an interview with a couple, he had determined that the husband was the primary financial decision-maker. Nonetheless, he proceeded with care, interacting as much (he thought) with the woman as with the man. The conversation seemed to go well, and he was optimistic that the couple would become clients. The next morning the husband called. "Felipe, I really want to work with you, but if I can talk my wife into coming back, you'd better make sure that you talk to her as much as to me. She felt discounted and not taken seriously as a client."

Felipe was stunned, but he was open to the possibility that his good intentions were mixed with biased assumptions and that he had, in fact, slighted the female client. Or perhaps her perception of equal attention was different from his. In either case, he was the one who needed to change.

In recent years, scientific research has emphasized the biological rather than the psychosocial reasons for gender differences. The most recent thrust of research, described for the layperson in *Brain Sex* by Ann Moir and David Jessel, seems to be that exposure to different levels of circulating testosterone before birth causes boys and girls to have different brain structures, which in turn translates into dissimilar thinking, communicating, and behaving.

A wide-ranging review of research in the March 27, 1995, issue of *Newsweek* points out that new brain imaging technologies demonstrate clear differences in how men's and women's brains actually function. Here are a few of the interesting findings:

• When asked to think about nothing, men think about sex and football, women think about the word "nothing."
• Men are better than women at reading maps.
• Women read emotions in people's faces better than men.
• Men's brains seem more channeled into one way of thinking and behaving than women's. Women's brains seem more channeled into multiple ways of thinking.

Even these new scientific findings have ramifications for the salesperson's adaptation to the gender of the consumer. If men and women really do think differently, then connecting with their way of thinking about purchases may be more difficult if you're a salesperson of the opposite sex.

Male-Female Differences in Communication

Whether the differences between the genders is derived from a biological or a sociological impetus, those differences are often most clearly manifested through communication. And communication is the primary vehicle that salespeople use to influence their customers. Knowing your own tendencies as a communicator as well as being able to assess the way your client communicates are essential in learning to adapt your style to your customer's style.

Common knowledge tells us that women generally prefer to talk about people, feelings, and relationships, while men prefer to talk about business, money, and sports. Women think more about products and services that will improve their connectedness with others. Their number one online activity is e-mail, a great demonstration of their interest in contacting, communicating, and connecting. Men are more likely to think in terms of doing, accomplishing, solving, or finishing a task. Often, the genders don't think highly of the topics the opposite sex prefers. In workshops that we conduct, men will often say they talk about substantive issues whereas women talk about trivia or gossip. Conversely, women will frequently say men just talk about things, not meaningful issues.

In an amusing example of gender differences, Dave Barry comments in his book *Dave Barry's Complete Guide to Guys* that men don't need or want to buy new clothes because they're so attached to their old ones. He says it is never okay to throw away veteran underwear. "A real guy checks the garbage regularly in case somebody—and we're not naming names, but this would be his wife—is quietly trying to discard his underwear, which she is frankly jealous of, because the guy seems to have a more intimate relationship with it than her."

Because women's and men's interests and communication vary, what they value in a sales context can be very different. In a long-term sales situation, such as buying a house, a woman may value more than anything else the perceived honesty and integrity of the salesperson, and the trusting association that she would like to develop and count on in the future. The man may instead value the salesperson's financial understanding, knowledge of construction pros and cons, and negotiating skills.

More important than the gender difference in *content* of communication is the *style* of communication during the actual sales process. Men tend to be competitive communicators. Women tend to be facilitative communicators. The outcomes that the genders are looking for in a conversation are often at odds. Men want to solve the problem, win the conversation, get it over with, and move on. Consequently, men often dominate conversations with women. They tell facts, give advice, and interrupt more frequently because they want to win, to come out on top. On the other hand, women's goal in communication is to understand and be understood. They want to be thorough and be sure that you as a salesperson are also thorough. They want and need time to get to know you and have you get to know them.

The *structure* of men's and women's communication is also very different. In answer to the question, "What are some female-male communication differences that you see in the workplace?" a recent workshop participant answered, "Men are all nouns and verbs, women are all adverbs and adjectives!" Indeed, this was a very graphic way of describing the differences in structure of communication.

Research reveals that women's conversation tends to be more detailed and descriptive than men's. They use qualifiers and disclaimers, apologies and explanations. They often start talking about a topic from the beginning rather than from the end; for example, if a salesperson asks a female customer about her needs relative to buying a computer, the customer might say, "Well, I've actually owned a variety of computers over more than ten years. I can't even remember the name of the company that made the first one I owned. They went out of business years ago. Actually, that's what forced me to get a second computer." This conversation could go on for a while before the customer arrived at the bottom line: "I need to use software that won't work on my present computer. That's why I need an upgrade."

Research confirms that men's conversational style tends to be concise, precise, and to the point. If you ask a man how he is or how the meeting went, he is more likely to say "Fine" than give you detail about the event or his feelings. Men see this interchange as a transaction that doesn't require much more information. If they are really intrigued with a topic or a problem, they are more inclined to talk much more elaborately and with detail.

As customers, men may sometimes respond so minimally that the salesperson has difficulty determining the exact needs without asking many more questions. If you ask a male customer the same question you asked a female customer, "What's your particular need right now in terms of computer capabilities?" he might say, "I need more memory," "I need more speed," or "I need more power." And you'll need more information.

Communicating Differently with Men or Women

If you have already been successful at selling specifically to one gender, there is every reason to believe you can double your sales revenue by increasing your sales to the other gender. Think about the possibility of selling as many retirement analyses to single women as to married men. Or selling cosmetics to men as well as women. Or selling subscriptions to *The Wall Street Journal* to as many women as men.

After you have assessed the gender characteristics of your client's communication and compared it with your own, you can plan the adaptations you'll need to be a more effective influencer. Remember the similarity bias. When you have common interests, when you speak in the language of your customers, they feel comfortable, liked, and are more readily influenced by you. That doesn't mean you have to speak with a southern accent if your client does, but it does mean that if your client is a slow, laid-back talker, you don't give her the high-powered, one hundred-mile-an-hour presentation that most people you've worked with love.

Sales Magic, an audiotape program by Kerry L. Johnson, takes the similarity principle even further by suggesting that the successful salesperson assesses the verbal and nonverbal components of her customer's style and models it exactly. If the customer crosses his legs, the salesperson crosses his legs. If the customer changes the pace of his conversation, the salesperson follows suit. The purpose? To subtly increase the customer's perception of similarity in order to increase the power of the salesperson's influence.

That kind of body language imitation wouldn't work well with opposite-sex salespeople and customers. Violations of sex role expectations would interfere with the desired outcome. Men sitting with legs crossed at the knee and hands folded in their lap, taking up little space and smiling frequently, as women often do, would in all likelihood seem odd. Similarly, women who take up a lot of space by crossing their legs with one ankle on the other knee, or by putting their arms up with their hands resting on the back of their head, would also seem a little strange. In verbal communication, however, there is plenty of room for narrowing the gap by adopting some characteristics of the other gender. These adaptations work in everyday communication as well as in sales.

The Gendersell Approach

Adaptive communication with the opposite sex is the foundation of the Gendersell approach. To "Gendersell" is *to use communication techniques typical of the other gender in order to increase potential for influence in sales situations.* We know that perceived similarity increases direct sales.

Raymond Miles, Ph.D., an organizational psychologist and professor in the School of Business at Berkeley, says that businesses today are entering the Age of Innovation in which they will focus on efficiently providing one-of-a-kind products or services to one-of-a-kind clients and needs. Mass production for mass markets is long gone. This same idea can be applied to selling. A highly specific approach customized to each individual client is what the Age of Innovation demands of its salespeople. A general approach to a general market will no longer work.

A recent article in *Selling* magazine about influencing customers in an international market asserts: "When in Rome, sell like the Romans." The Gendersell approach suggests, "When selling to a male, sell more like a man," and "When selling to a woman, sell more like a woman."

In his recent book *The Platinum Rule,* Tony Alessandra asserts, "We need to think in the language of our customer." The Gendersell program raises this bar a notch higher: Salespeople need to *talk* in the language of their customer. When we speak in our customer's language, they perceive us as similar to them—and similarity breeds trust.

One minute after a male customer walks in the door of a jewelry store, the female salesperson needs to make some educated guesses about what the man's needs are. Is he buying for himself or someone else? Is he a practical or an extravagant person? She needs to watch where he goes and what he is looking at, rather than ask the standard "May I help you?" (Men rarely respond positively to this question for the same reason that they rarely stop to ask for directions when lost.) When the customer pauses in front of a counter and appears to be looking at a piece of jewelry, make a comment like "You seem to have good taste in jewelry. I'm Mary Robinson, the senior sales consultant." Then offer and give a warm handshake. To your male customer this is a business transaction, a problem to be solved, a task to be accomplished. Usually, men go buying, not shopping. The saleswoman needs to act and communicate differently with this male customer than she would a female customer.

A female customer is more likely to respond favorably to a helping approach: "Is there something in particular you're looking for, or would you like to browse awhile?" The female customer may just want to look, without buying anything at all. She may be enjoying a brief respite in her frantic day, rewarding herself with a few moments of luxury looking. Because the female customer is not quite as task oriented as her male counterpart, she may be more open to some general conversation: about the weather, the traffic, or a genuine compliment about jewelry she is wearing. Demonstrating that you take her seriously as a customer means introducing yourself and perhaps shaking hands, conveying acceptance that she is looking rather than buying, encouraging her to come back and browse, and telling her when you usually work.

On a day when the Dow Jones dropped more than a hundred points, a new young, male stockbroker used a brilliant Gendersell approach. He called all the women on a list of previous Merrill Lynch clients and asked if they would be interested in a very safe low-risk investment in short- and long-term CDs that he could offer them today at a decent interest rate. He applied what he knew about many women and money: Women are less confident of their investment decisions, want advice, and are more conservative than men. He didn't call the men on the list because he thought they would be more likely to tough out the situation, rather than acknowledge possible fear of financial risk.

These scenarios illustrate selling one-to-one, emphasizing gender as the specific variable for adaptation. But because all men and all women are not the same, the salesperson needs to continue refining the process to fit the unique customer within each gender category.

What Other Adaptations Need to Happen?

Are there other factors involved in the sales transaction besides the similarity bias and the gender variable? Definitely, as the conclusion to my (Judy's) car-buying story illustrates. I ended up buying the car from Joe, the male salesperson, despite that fact that I was totally annoyed with his tactics by the end of the month. As it turned out, Dorothy had left her dealership during this time period, and no other representative from that organization ever attempted to contact me. Joe won a war of attrition, although I won't return to that dealership for my next car. Timing, cost, investment, and availability are all variables that affect what and when we buy. But barring those, customers choose to buy from someone they perceive is on their wavelength, who speaks the same language.

When timing and communication aren't going well, when you can tell you've missed the similarity connection between you and the customer, the best strategy may be to withdraw, review, and reevaluate the situation's potential. Fran, the owner of an advertising agency, was about to present a major campaign to the CEO of a large household products company. She had been working diligently for two months to put this presentation together. Before she began, she overheard fragments of quietly urgent conversation with references to stock price drop, rumors about merger, and replacement of senior management. When the corporate group assembled, they were clearly unfocused. She said, "Gentlemen, I have the feeling this isn't the best time for our presentation. I would be happy to reschedule if that would work for you." The CEO agreed, obviously relieved at her apparent empathy. The rescheduled meeting took place without a hitch, and Fran got the business. Recalling the first meeting, the CEO took Fran aside and said, "I knew you'd be right. Anybody *that* perceptive and *that* flexible has to be good."

Adaptations are part of every phase of selling. What stages are most integral when selling to one sex or the other? When is the right time to start closing? When and with whom should you ask more, and when should you tell more? What is the best way to introduce yourself to men and to women? When do you focus on the process, and when do you focus on the product? The answer to all of these questions depends on the customer, on the product or service you're selling, on your perceptiveness, and on the situation and the context. Selling an office building to a woman who has owned multiple office complexes is totally different from selling to a man who has never bought real estate of any type. Selling stocks or bonds over the phone to women is very different from selling long-distance phone service to a man.

At every first contact with a customer the salesperson needs to be in high perception-absorption gear—continuously listening, observing, sensing, recognizing, and modifying. Appreciating the stimulation of difference in every sales situation, the challenge of versatility, the excitement of multiple opportunities, and the driving demand of many diverse customers can renew even the most experienced salesperson's passion and energy.

Traditionally, selling has been a male game of winning or losing. You play hard to win, you follow certain rules, but you get away with what you can. You're tough, you're aggressive, and you don't take any crap from your opponents. You do whatever it takes to gain those yards, to get within scoring range, to win the game. When it's over, it's over. Whether you have won or lost, you don't think back and obsess. You just get ready for the next game.

In today's market, however, the successful salesperson is a synchronized swimmer, a doubles tennis player, or a relay racer rather than a football, baseball, or basketball player. He or she is a partner, a team player, a collaborator, or an advocate, not an adversary. And the ascendant sales pro is always working on learning, enhancing, and improving his skills in selling to the opposite sex.

Move to the Future

For lovemaking advice, would you turn to a book written in the nineteenth century? The idea is preposterous. But strangely enough, many of today's books about sales repeat the advice that may have been innovative in 1930 but is old, tired, and untrue today.

Customers have changed just as corporate cultures have changed in the face of today's global economy. From the airline passenger who asks for a glass of water, diet Coke with a slice of lime, and three bags of peanuts instead of one, to the female patient who insists on seeing a female rather than a male physician, consumers want more customization.

Getting rid of the old and trying on the new isn't all that tough. There are challenges and opportunities in moving into the next century of successful selling. It's exciting, profitable, and even fun.

Chapter 3
Men Influencing Women

Men in sales seem to know the answers to all customer questions. They can quote statistics and communicate a myriad of facts. They can dispense sizes and shapes, radii and circumferences, square feet and cubic centimeters. Many of them can rattle on about gigabites and rpms, torque and debentures, and with enthusiasm that few women can match. And for the most part our research supports the belief that men are more informed than women about products and service—particularly technical, mechanical, quantitative "stuff." While the male sales professional was viewed as a font of information, the major drawback of women in sales, as revealed by the Sales Preference Survey, was a lack of product knowledge.

Perhaps some fundamental differences between the genders are the basis for the perception of the product knowledge gap. A caller to *Car Talk,* the funny National Public Radio car fix-it program, asked what the difference was between rpm and torque. As a salesman new to car sales, the caller had been taught to rely heavily on product knowledge to talk customers into a purchase. He acknowledged that he didn't know much but had been instructed to throw a lot of heavy jargon around to impress his customers with his expertise. After a particularly elaborate speech, his male customer asked him about the difference between rpm and torque. The salesman told the *Car Talk* hosts that he had no inkling, but since he had set himself up as an expert, he couldn't possibly admit the truth to the customer.

The advice-giving brothers on *Car Talk,* humor in hand, said,

"Well, I always think honesty is the best policy—except in car sales, of course." The serious point they made was that the salesman shouldn't throw around terms he doesn't understand because he risks setting himself up to be challenged by a competitor or misleading someone who is genuinely looking for information.

Women in sales would be less inclined to follow the "show but no know" approach than men—and not necessarily because they're more honest. In fact, because many fear being caught with the wrong answer, they choose to focus on their people and process skills.

The number one drawback of male sales professionals, according to our research, was that men are "too pushy and aggressive." Some of the comments were "They're high pressure and in a hurry," "They can be overbearing and devious," "They're intimidating," and "They don't give you time to think through the sale." Male respondents cited male salespeople's lack of sincerity and honesty as the number two disadvantage. Few men saw any other disadvantages.

Female respondents noted the number two drawback about men in sales was that they acted superior, had too much ego, and were condescending. Women in high numbers mentioned men's insensitivity to customer needs, their impatience and lack of politeness, and their poor listening skills in addition to their pushiness.

Women Want to Be Taken Seriously

Women's primary concern as customers is being taken seriously. They want to be treated as a respected, valued, intelligent, and financially able consumer. A survey reported in the June 1996 newsletter *About Women and Marketing* concluded that women elicit less respect than men in a whole host of day-to-day encounters, including buying a house, buying a car, and going to a car mechanic for repairs.

Recently, a friend, Rosalee, went to a piano store to arrange piano lessons as a gift for her husband. She is a bright, capable person but is piano illiterate. In the course of asking a variety of questions, she asked the salesman, "Are there ways for people to practice while they are taking lessons other than by renting a piano?" She was picturing a new technology for novices that would allow keyboard practice or even computer practice of some sort to substitute for an actual piano. The salesperson looked quite puzzled and responded, "Well, I just wouldn't know if that was possible or not. If you're going to learn to play the piano, I'd think you'd have to practice. And I'd think you'd have to practice on something like a piano, wouldn't you?" Without waiting for a reply, he called another salesperson over and asked, "Jim, this nice lady wants to know if there are other ways to practice piano without renting a piano. Do you have any good ideas?" Not surprisingly, Rosalee did not feel that she had been taken seriously as a customer and left the store.

This is an example of the double whammy—two-time condescension. The comments of the salesperson were extremely off-putting in the first place, but the belief that his female customer wouldn't pick up on his tone and attitude was even more offensive. The salesperson lost lessons, piano rental, and probably a future piano sale in three minutes.

Male consumers are not usually so concerned about not being taken seriously as customers. Accurately or not, they generally feel they are treated with respect. As in other relationships, men are less apt to take things personally and are less apt to express their feelings of discomfort or dissatisfaction.

Most men in sales need to focus more on the process of building the sales relationship and less on the product or service being sold if they want to increase their success with female customers. Survey after survey has demonstrated that a broad spectrum of women want to be treated more respectfully, would like to inhabit a more caring world, and have a higher need than men to connect with others. By understanding what women want as customers, by moving less quickly and aggressively, and by genuinely adapting to the female differences in thinking, communicating, shopping, and buying, the male salesperson can achieve impressive results.

The following tips are ways for men to give their female customers the treatment they want. They will help you to keep building the relationship even after you have started giving heavy product information or making a presentation. Don't forget to view your female customer as a person, not just a potential purchaser, and to give continued attention to her needs and wants.

Giving Female Customers What They Want

Although most sales books written by men for men emphasize establishing a relationship with the customer, the specifics of relationship building with women are drastically different. For many women the relationship and customer service are more important than the product or price. Consequently, working at building rapport, establishing trust, and identifying the female customer's needs and wants well before you even begin to talk about the product is the effective approach to take.

Mark Edgerton, a principal of FiestaNet, a company that designs and maintains Web pages for small businesses, government agencies, and not-for-profit organizations, spends his first meeting with a potential female customer by introducing her to the other employees who might be involved in her project and educating her about how his company can best provide the quality and effectiveness that she wants in her Web site.

Lola, a small-business owner, was investigating the possibility of setting up a Web page on the Internet. She made an appointment with Mark, whom she knew slightly through volunteer work. Mark spent an hour educating Lola, asking about her needs, and suggesting the steps to take over time in a relaxed, comfortable manner.

He introduced her to his colleagues and explained their roles in her potential project. There was no push, no press. Only when asked did he quote prices for creating and maintaining the Web site.

Shortly thereafter a friend told Lola that she knew about a company which would do the same thing for half of what Mark's company quoted. But Lola wasn't even interested in finding out more. Mark's low-key, educational, partnering approach was more valuable to her than saving money.

In a personal relationship with a woman, most men know that a fair amount of rapport and relationship building has to precede the pitch. The same principle is true in sales. If a female customer is buying a new refrigerator for her house or a new telephone system for her office, she wants to know you, trust you, and to have you understand her before you press the deal.

Introduce yourself, look your customer in the eye, and shake her hand. It's the best way to begin a business relationship. Shaking hands is an excellent way to convey the impression that you take the customer seriously as a businessperson. A sales situation of any kind is a business transaction, and both of you—the salesperson and the customer—need to act in a businesslike, professional way. However, the burden of proof and professionalism is always on the salesperson.

A couple seeking estate planning advice was shopping for a lawyer. The man, Reed, didn't much care which lawyer they went to; he saw the task as unpleasant and time-consuming, and just wanted to get done. Marta, on the other hand, felt they were choosing a lifetime consultant on extremely important issues—money, life, and death. She generally preferred to seek the advice of women. In the matter of estate planning, she decided that she felt more confident with a man, but she was dubious about his ability to take her seriously, focus on both her and her husband, and share the same vision she had of creating a long-term relationship.

The lawyer passed the initial test by shaking hands with both clients, looking Marta in the eye, and asking questions that reflected his awareness that although they were a couple, Reed and Marta might have entirely different thoughts, needs, or concerns about their estate. "Reed, what outcome would you like from our meeting today?" "Marta, what's your primary concern in terms of estate planning?" The lawyer continued to demonstrate to Marta that he was interested in establishing a long-term relationship. He always took the time to answer her telephone questions at no fee; he often answered his phone personally and occasionally even took the initiative to call and see how Marta was doing on information preparation for their meetings.

Your female customer will want to know who you are, and she'll want to test your handshake. Limp handshakes don't work well with women in this country (although in many other countries a limp handshake from men or women is much more acceptable than in the United States). Bone-crushing handshakes don't work well, either. Of course, shaking hands may not always be the best tactic, but as a general rule it's a good idea. However, don't rely on the old rule to wait and see if the woman takes the initiative. Unless there is a strong clue to the contrary, behave as you would in any business transaction: Introduce yourself and shake hands.

Depending on the situation, the next step is to ask your female customer if she has time to talk for a few minutes so you can find out what she's looking for and what her specific needs are. It doesn't matter what you call this process—doing a needs assessment, information gathering, making small talk, identifying your customer's unique style—but this step is crucial when building a relationship with your female customer. It is primarily here that you will win her or lose her.

The CEO of a printing company recently recalled an appointment ten years ago with a loan officer at a major bank. She remembered clearly that he never looked her in the eye when he talked to her. That one incident not only discouraged her from dealing with him, but she also avoided male loan officers and lending institutions altogether. There are many similar stories out there from women who remember poor relationship-building skills.

To build a relationship with a female customer:

• Introduce yourself, shake hands, look the customer in the eye, and convey that you take her seriously as a customer.

• Focus first on her purchase needs and wants rather than on the product or service.

• Take the time to determine what she wants from you in the sales relationship process before you begin to talk about the product or service.

• Earn her trust. Be consistent, honest, and helpful in the way she wants to be helped.

Go Slowly

When women are about to spend a lot of money on a car, a house, health insurance, or a financial investment, they often proceed far more slowly than men. They want to shop and make comparisons. When it comes to money, they have a lower risk-taking propensity. They generally want to be thoroughly educated about the product or service they are buying.

If women don't come to the sales situation already well informed, they'll look to the salesperson or the company to give them information. Women prefer that educational information be separate from selling information in written and verbal material. Therefore, handing out a brochure about how to select a financial adviser would be separate from a conversation about why a certain broker or company would be best.

Unfortunately, many men perceive women's propensity to ask many questions as a sign of weakness and respond in ways that result in their feeling patronized. Delivering complex information slowly but not necessarily too simply is the key. For example, Bob, a friendly computer software fellow who was supposed to make computers understandable for everyone, was not successful because his approach was so slow and simple that even computer novices were insulted.

The large quantity of information desired and gathered by women can make the decision-making process slower as more facts and feelings are figured into the equation. However, this lengthy, informed process of shopping is often the preferred female way to buy.

A group of women business owners who met monthly for leads often asked each other for suggestions about business equipment and services. "Who do you use for computer repair services?" "Where did you buy your car?" "Who do you use for your corporate financial planning?" "What long-distance carrier do you prefer?" "What's the best plain paper fax?" Even when specific phone numbers and names of sales or service people were given with strong references, they often would not complete the transaction for a month or more. Why? Because they needed more time to talk to more people to gather more facts and opinions.

A CEO of a company that sells vacation homes recently asked me (Judy) why a higher percentage of women initially agree to buy but then a higher percentage also change their mind and back out of the deal. My guess is that the women are being pressured at the same rate as the men, but the pace is too fast for them. They say yes before they have had time to really think about it; they agree as a way to back off and regroup or to avoid rejecting the salesperson. With time, they decide against the purchase. I think slowing the sales pace would decrease the immediate yes but decrease the later no.

Expecting the difference in pace and not pressuring works like a charm. In most instances, making the sale will take you longer with a woman than a man. The stereotypical car salesperson's standard question—"What would it take to get you to buy the car today?"—shouldn't even be asked of women. She will not buy the car today even if she trusts you, and she will never buy it if you ask this question early in the sales interaction. It is better to ask her what her timetable is for making the decision and plan accordingly.

You may lose a sale by being fast and attentive with a female customer. You may lose it by being slow and inattentive. But you'll never lose it by being slow and attentive. If you are attentive and she happens to be someone who wants a faster sales process, she'll let you know, and you can pick up the pace.

Going slowly means you should

• look at the sales situation with a woman as a process, not an event;
• let the female customer set the pace for the sales process and respond to her cues to move to the next stage of selling;
• give her information in verbal and written form, with time to think, ask, review, and validate;
• separate education from selling;
• not pressure or push for a decision.

Listen

Men are tired of hearing from women that they don't listen well. Because men don't listen or respond in the same way women do, women assume that listening isn't happening even when men are tuned in. The next time you are in a sales situation or even a social situation, notice the differences in how men and women respond verbally and nonverbally when they are truly listening to other people's words.

Our gender styles as listeners are amazingly different. When men listen to men, they are often shoulder to shoulder and may not look at each other. They often have minimal eye contact. They rarely nod their heads and often don't respond with any com-

ment—not even "uh-huh." This won't work with female customers; women will feel that you are listening if you appear attentive. Change facial expression occasionally, nod your head, ask
more about what she said, acknowledge what she said, paraphrase
what she said, or reflect the feelings she is expressing. Interaction
is key for women.

Larry sells solutions. He is proud of the fact that his greatest
skill is problem-solving related to hardware and software needs of
businesses. He is experienced, knowledgeable, and intelligent. He
is a good communicator and can turn technical lingo into understandable messages. But the women who seek his advice see only
his seemingly quick read of their needs; his apparent assumption
that he knows the problem and the solution before they have even
finished describing the situation; his interruption of them to tell
them that he has the answer; and his quickness in forming a plan.
In essence, they think he hasn't listened to them. They want to be
able to finish their story. They want some acknowledgment, some
head nodding, some empathy, some patience, some time.

If in the future a woman tells you that you are not listening,
don't deny her accusation. Instead, recognize that she is in effect
saying, "You're not listening to me in the same way I listen to you.
I want you to listen to me the way I listen to you." Reframing her
statement may help you become more open-minded about responding in a way she will appreciate. Improving your listening—
or at least attaining the perception that you are listening—is
probably the single most important action that you can take to increase your success with female customers. When they feel listened to, women feel they are being taken seriously.

In his book *Leader Effectiveness Training,* Dr. Thomas Gordon
describes "active listening skills" that almost force you to slow
your pace. They consist of **paraphrasing, reflecting the feeling,**
and **restating.** Each can be used in any phase of the sales process,
but with women it is best to implement them at the beginning.
These techniques demonstrate understanding and interest in what

the customer is thinking and feeling, and encourage her to give you more information.

By **paraphrasing,** the sales professional puts the customer's original comment in his own words. For example, the customer might say to the salesman, "I'm interested in a camera that does it all for me." To paraphrase, the salesperson could say, "You're interested in one of the new fully automatic models." This gives the customer the chance to validate or disagree with your reading of her message. She can agree or may say, "Well, it doesn't have to be a new model, but I do want one that is mostly automatic. I just don't take good pictures." Although you are not asking a question, you will obtain information that will be helpful without sounding as if you are interrogating her.

Next, if you are really agile, you can move into **reflecting the feeling** by acknowledging the apparent emotion in the buyer's statement. Again, you are communicating interest, attention, and concentration to the customer. In this situation you might say, "Sounds as if you are a little discouraged about photography" or "You're hoping the automatic model will upgrade your picture-taking abilities." Using these feeling words will encourage your customer to tell you more.

Restating is another form of active listening. In essence, it's an interrogative spin on the customer's own words. The purpose is to buy time, to encourage the customer to elaborate, and to let her know that you are paying attention. For example, the customer might say, "I'm not really ready to make the final decision about the funeral arrangements today." Rather than saying, "When will you be ready?" or "Why aren't you ready?" simply restate: "You're not ready today." This will encourage her to say more without more questions on your part. She may say, perhaps, "I need to talk to my sister, and she won't be in town until tomorrow" or "I'm still overwhelmed by all that has happened." In either case, you are armed with more information that you can use supportively rather than coming across as cold or uncaring.

Two or three rounds of active listening, along with some head nods and eye contact, will convey empathy—a powerful way to gather data and increase the customer's perception that you and she are on the same wavelength. This puts you in a good position to begin asking some more highly focused questions.

Good listening is demonstrated by

- eye contact and occasional head nodding and/or saying "uh-huh";
- avoiding interruption of the customer;
- using active listening skills: paraphrasing, reflection of feeling, and restatement;
- conveying genuine empathy when you can.

Building a relationship, going slow, and listening are the three main techniques that can increase men's success in selling to women. The following tips are fine-tuning steps that will solidify the relationship.

Ask More, Tell Less

As a sales or service professional, giving facts, information, advice, and suggestions is an important part of the job. But you should proceed with caution: Burdening female customers with unasked for information, unsolicited advice, opinions, beliefs, numbers, and data often elicits a negative response.

The classic overload situation occurs in the presence of three factors: high-tech equipment, a technically knowledgeable salesperson, and a technically illiterate female customer. Are there also technically illiterate male customers? Yes. Would the "ask more, tell less" approach work with them? Not necessarily. Men would be more likely to perceive a salesperson who doesn't tell as a salesperson who doesn't know. But men might also leave the situation rather than reveal their lack of know-how.

Here is the common overload situation:

LELEELA (looking at printer in computer store): Hmm.

STERLING (salesperson): Are there any questions I can answer for you about this particular printer?

LELEELA (not knowing what to ask): Not really.

STERLING (figuring she doesn't know enough to ask, so he'll just tell her and help her out): This is the top of the line—really the best model we sell. The imaging technology allows it to scale outline printer fonts provided with the printer up to 250 points, and also rotate fonts at arbitrary angles. The interface not only recognizes the tbpp network but also serial connections. In serial mode the baud rate is 57.6, 8 bit, no parity.

Is that dialogue made up? Yes—because customers who hear that type of communication never understand it and so can't repeat it. But they generally respond in the same way: They buy elsewhere.

Politeness and manners in conversation are more important to women than to men. Research consistently finds that women are concerned about civility, about living in a kinder, more caring world. Their communication style is gentler. Make yours the same. Softening the probe helps: "Would you mind telling me . . ." "Is it okay to sit in my office for a few minutes while we talk rather than standing out here?" "Would you like a cup of coffee while we're talking?" These are all hospitable approaches.

Act in Accord

Give the female customer what she says she wants and needs rather than try to convince her otherwise. Genuinely fit the product or service to the female customer rather than vice versa. Long-held tradition sometimes makes men act as if they know what is best for women, despite the women's protestations to the contrary.

Marlissa, a psychologist, was looking for office space. She told Sam, the male realtor, that she wanted an airy, open, garden-like office building and lots of windows in her office. His response? "You don't want a lot of windows. Your patients are going to want privacy. They don't want people looking in on them and staring at them." Even when Marlissa justified her desire—"I'll have blinds, of course, but when I'm working in the office alone, I like to be able to look out at the trees and shrubs and see the sky instead of feeling closed in"—Mike insisted his view was the right one. "Your patients will want a nice private, dark place, not a bright, open place." What happened? A lost sale. Marlissa found another realtor—one who acted in accord with her, not in opposition to her.

It is important to identify your customer's interests and what she is looking for in a product or service rather than what you might want or what you might have available. This is a strong way to build trust in the relationship while conveying that you take the female customer seriously.

Talk About People and the Product or Service

Use your information gathering as a basis for talking about the service or product as something that the customer and others will be using and enjoying: "Your kids will enjoy the games capability of the computer." "Does your husband or the children have similar or different ideas as to what they want in the new family car?" "Your mother will enjoy the safety features as well." "This is a great way to liven up your Mexican party. We'll find some good mariachi music for you to play on the new compact disc player."

This kind of discussion works better than talking about all the great features of the car, of the financial services, of the CD player, or of the computer as an inanimate object. For women, the purchased product or service is meant in some way or other to improve the people, feelings, and relationship issues in their business or personal lives.

Increase the Use of Feeling Words and Emotional Events

Try to talk about feelings—yours as well as your female customer's and those of similar customers; for example, "I just ran into a customer who bought an SUV like this from me six months ago. She's an accountant who is also a grandparent. She's so enthusiastic. She said she felt really comfortable driving her grandkids around in such a safe, dependable car."

Since many women prefer to talk about people, feelings, and relationships, linking your product or service to your female customer's areas of interest will work well. It doesn't need to be a forced, excessive reach. You don't have to match her level of emotionality or intensity about these topics, but moving away from facts and data works well.

A colleague, Liz, recently decided to go car shopping because she liked a new friend's automobile. She liked the way it drove, the way it looked, and the way it felt when she was a passenger. She didn't know much about it except the make. When she went into the dealership, she told the salesperson that she liked her friend's car and wanted to look around. He responded by trying to establish the exact kind of car her friend had: "Is it an XZE346T or is it the KLP890X? Is it a V-8 or a 6? Is it the sedan deluxe LX or the MX?"

Liz didn't know and didn't care, but she felt interrogated and stupid in this process. While her way of thinking about cars was perhaps different from the standard "man's" way, the fact that she doesn't know model numbers doesn't mean she is dumb. She left quickly and didn't return.

A much better approach for the salesperson would have been to ask what Liz liked about her friend's car or what her friend liked about the car. After this, an inquiry could be made about Liz's particular needs and wants. Next, he could fit those feelings, needs, and wants to the car and model. She may end up buying a model completely different from her friend's because it doesn't matter what make or model it is as long as she gets the same feeling and experience that she had in her friend's car.

A similar tale concerns a doctor who wanted to purchase new office space. She ultimately chose a building shown by a realtor who quickly caught the *feeling* of what she wanted: "I want my patients to feel relaxed, easy, and comfortable when they come to see me. I don't want the building to be threatening or overwhelming." The realtor found one that fit the feeling: a small, rambling, vine-covered, one-story brick building with a shingled roof and lots of parking. She had probably not used any of those words to describe the building she wanted, but he sure caught on to the feeling she wanted.

Avoid Giving Advice Unless Asked

Women often take well-intentioned suggestions as attempts to control or be patronizing. Men often see themselves as problem-solvers and fixers. Conversely, women tend to communicate information in order to help you understand their perspective, not to fix it. For example, a female customer might comment that the fax machine she is contemplating buying appears somewhat complex. The salesperson might understandably launch into some reassuring dialogue, followed by instructions about the simplicity of operating the machine. But the female customer might have preferred some empathy, such as, "At first a plain paper fax may seem complex, but once you become familiar with it, I think you'll find its versatility a tremendous advantage."

It is better to wait until you're asked for advice or, better, *ask* your female customer if she'd like a suggestion or an opinion: "Would you be interested in my opinion about the advantages of the plain paper fax over the thermal fax?" or "Would you like me to run through the operation of this fax briefly with you?"

When the Sale Is Over, Keep in Touch

For many women an ongoing relationship is part of the successful sales process. If you want a female customer to be a customer for life, keep in touch, paying attention to her as an individual. Do it by phone or with cards or notes; send an article on a topic of interest to her. Don't send a generic "Happy Birthday"; instead, take the time to write "Hope you and Eric can take a few days off and go to your new cabin to celebrate your birthday!" As a rule, women don't feel they are being taken seriously as customers unless there is follow-up.

Accept That Women Are Higher Maintenance Than Men as Customers

An article by Emma Hall describes advertising agencies' difficulties in portraying women in ways that are acceptable to them. The implication is that selling to women is complicated. "Women are keen to be targeted by advertisers but are ultrasensitive about being patronized," Hall notes.

Just as selling to someone from a different country may be more work, selling to women is often tougher for men than selling to men. Mike Errico, quoted in a *Newsweek* article called "Bad

Boys," commented, "It's just so goddamn exhausting to be sensitive" when dealing with women. But by understanding the woman as a consumer better, by realizing she is different and that her difference isn't a deficiency, and by increasing gender-specific techniques, men can tap into the huge market of female consumers. These consumers have lots of money to spend, lots of power to make decisions, and lots of choices about where to buy.

A male sales professional doesn't have to turn into a female to be successful with female clients. He can acquire some of the qualities valued in female salespeople: integrity, perceptiveness about client and customer needs, good conversation skills—including listening—a broad repertoire of communication techniques, and a genuine interest in the customer and a long-term relationship. A judicious use of these techniques will benefit *every* salesperson.

Chapter 4
Women Influencing Men

The following experience illustrates what the Customer Preference Survey revealed as an asset in female sales professionals when it came to meeting client needs. Linda Kaplan is a sharp and savvy marketing consultant who was invited to join the sales department of an upscale automobile dealership. Shortly after she joined the dealership, a male customer wanted to buy a specific model of a car in brown. Although there were no brown vehicles on the lot, Linda wanted to give the customer the color he wanted. Meanwhile, the sales manager was urging her to sell the customer on a green model they had in stock. Undaunted, Linda insisted on putting in the extra effort and made calls to dealerships near and far to find the model and color the customer wanted. Through her persistence in meeting this customer's needs and wants, Linda received several strong referrals, the powerful word-of-mouth phenomenon began to snowball, and she quickly built a loyal clientele that would not deal with anyone in the dealership but her. Her happy customers knew that she had their best interests at heart. One wonders how many customers have been lost because some shortsighted sales manager wanted to "move the inventory."

Our research indicates that women in sales often excel at creating rapport and establishing relationships. They are persistent and detail-oriented, and they communicate well. Female sales professionals have taste and creativity, aren't pushy or self-absorbed, and generally put client needs first and foremost. Women sales professionals want to make their customer feel that their every wish will be granted. Maxine, a top producer in the insurance industry, attributed her success to diligence and true caring. "I consider myself kind and empathetic," she said. "And although I may get clients more slowly than others, I tend to keep them."

While female sales professionals were viewed as experts in "people knowledge," the survey also revealed a perceived lack of product knowledge:

"Women don't seem as knowledgeable in a male-dominated business."

"Don't have all the info needed. Maybe too timid."

"Don't understand technical issues."

"Don't understand male logic."

"Less likely to make a recommendation and usually not mechanically inclined."

"Unsure of the product."

"Lack of knowledge/mechanics; don't consider value versus cost."

The good news, however, is that immediate action can effectively counteract the negative image.

Building Credibility

Know Your Product

In chapter 3 we discussed the fact that men are good at quantitative information: facts, sizes and shapes, radii, square feet, rpms, torque, and debentures. Understanding one of the basic gender communication differences—that men like to talk about things and facts while women like to talk about people and feelings—can help a female sales professional build credibility with her male

customers. Understanding your product thoroughly and being prepared to give facts and data when the customer wants that type of
information is the surest way to overcome this barrier.

When Linda started selling automobiles, she didn't know a
suspension system from a steering radius. To turn this weak point
into a strength, she decided to spend several days in the service department. She asked questions. She put on her Levi's and got under
the cars. She asked the mechanic to point out the underside work-
ings of the automobiles. She raised the hood and asked more questions. She had a service manager point out the features and
benefits, and explain what functions each part performed. Within
days she learned the concepts and language she needed to do her
job well. Eventually she could speak with knowledge when someone asked, "What makes this vehicle safer than others?" Her male
customers, in particular, responded enthusiastically to her level of
product knowledge and quickly forgot the gender issue when they
realized Linda knew what she was talking about. They were impressed.

There is no substitute for product knowledge, particularly
when you're working with male customers. Bite the bullet, get
down and dirty, hire a tutor or a mentor or a coach—but learn the
facts. It is also important for a female sales professional to discern
the level of knowledge of her male customer. For the same reason
that men hesitate to ask for directions, they are not quick to admit
that they don't know something.

Tony was purchasing a vacuum cleaner. He didn't know exactly what to ask for; he just knew he had to have a good one since
he had just had his house recarpeted. Sheila, who had excellent
product knowledge as a sales professional, saw Tony looking at an
expensive vacuum cleaner and remarked, "That model is a beauty,
isn't she? It's the latest in carpet-cleaning technology. What model
do you presently own?"

Tony was thinking, "A blue one," but rather than reveal his ig-
norance and risk his macho image by engaging in small talk about

his current vacuum, he walked away, commenting, "Oh, I'm just looking." Tony needed to save face.

Some men would rather "walk" than reveal their lack of information. In this case, Sheila's product knowledge actually got her in trouble. Knowing *when* to bring in the facts and data, and just *how fast* to cover the basic information is just as important as the product knowledge itself. Always find out discreetly what level of product knowledge your customer has and then move forward at his pace.

Begin by asking questions that ease into the conversation: Do you have carpeting in the house or area rugs? Do you have a thick carpet or a tight weave? Do you have children? Will you be the primary user of the vacuum, or will other people use it as well? By asking open-ended, low-risk questions and letting the customer lead the product knowledge dance, the female sales professional can position herself as an amiable, nonthreatening guide in the sales process.

Take a Confident Tone

Interestingly, Linda noted that *acting* as if you know what you are talking about is just as important as the actual product knowledge. One can have good product knowledge, but if it is presented in a tentative, apologetic, or unprofessional way, it will not build credibility.

An aura of confidence has a number of specific characteristics: a strong voice, persuasive words, solid eye contact, and fluid and dynamic body language. The resulting image is professional. The attitude is positive and enthusiastic. Confidence is a by-product of hands-on experience, combined with comfort level, product knowledge, and belief in the product or service being sold. The customer's trust in the female sales professional's expertise is thereby increased.

Danielle Kennedy, the award-winning real estate salesperson and motivational speaker, says that she creates a market position low on hype and high on experience. She tells her audiences: "I sold more real estate in ten years than most salespeople sell in a lifetime. I want to share my experience with you to prevent your team from making unnecessary mistakes." This woman has experience, uses it, and addresses the credibility issue up front in her speeches, workshops, and marketing materials.

When you know what you are talking about, you can help the customer in ways they don't anticipate. While selling a sales seminar to a male meeting planner who was newly in charge of his association's annual convention, I (Lee) asked who some of his primary exhibitors were. "Well, I hadn't really thought about having exhibitors," he responded. "This is primarily an educational convention."

I told him that an association can actually *make* money on a convention and bring in better educational programming by selling booth space to vendors who want visibility for their products. This also helps attendees acquaint themselves with the latest and best products and services in their industry. The organization makes money, and the vendors love the exposure. It is a total win-win proposition.

The client was excited and grateful for this information, and he subsequently asked for advice on a variety of other issues: agenda, audio and video recording of the events, other speakers and seminar leaders, and special tours. It became clear that my experience and knowledge of the meetings industry could help his association make money *and* help him over the hurdles in his new job. I became an information resource to him, a consultant rather than a peddler. After I helped him solve problems he hadn't even contemplated, selling him on the idea of buying educational services was a slam dunk. He was soon delighted to talk about my sales training services.

Use Business, Money, and Sports Terminology

Patricia was giving a sales training presentation for a well-known high-tech corporation. The audience of twenty people was predominantly male. The discussion revolved around leadership, setting a good example, and being a good role model. Chicago Bulls basketball player Dennis Rodman was mentioned as a controversial role model.

When Patricia innocently asked, "Who is Dennis Rodman?" there was dead silence from the audience, and then they burst into an uproar: "You don't know who Dennis Rodman is? You're kidding, aren't you?" Patricia quickly lost credibility with her male audience. She may have known about her product, but to know so little about something of great interest to her male audience seemed unforgivable.

It doesn't take major research to discover that the three topics men are most interested in are business, money, and sports, and it is crucial that female sales professionals be well read, knowledgeable, and informed on all issues relevant to their male customers. In this case, Patricia failed to understand a sports basic, and she therefore lost an audience of potential sale. Resolving never to let a similar incident happen again, Patricia began to read the headlines of the sports section every morning. She made sure she knew which sport season it was, who the major teams were, and what stories were making the headlines.

From then on, when selling to men, Patricia always made a point of making some reference to a sports figure or telling some current story about the hometown team. Besides improving her rate of sales with men, a surprising thing happened: Patricia started to *enjoy* following sports events, and eventually she was able to root for her favorite teams along with the guys.

In any sales situation, knowing which interests are important to your customer and including that information as a rapport builder increases the likelihood of a connection. This same rule applies as far as being informed on the stock market or what is going on in the world of business. We are often amazed at how much more easily conversations are initiated by men when we carry copies of *The Wall Street Journal* to meetings or on business trips. We are automatically perceived as being "in the know."

Get to the Bottom Line

When a woman is selling an idea, product, or service to a man, it is important to get to the main point early and quickly in the conversation. Give the facts, then fill in the details later. Avoid detailed explanations, disclaimers, and qualifiers: "We *probably* should do this." "It *seems* like a fairly good concept."

Marilyn, on the same sales team as Dave, would go into Dave's office with her creative ideas and "think out loud." She noticed that Dave's eyes would quickly start to glaze over, and she felt she was "losing him." Marilyn would then start talking faster and in more detail to convince him that her idea had merit. But the more she tried to explain, the more Dave appeared distracted.

Instead of "You know, I've been thinking about the Conant account, and it seems to me that something doesn't feel quite right. It's as if something has changed, but I'm not sure what it is. They seemed more gung ho last year, and I'm starting to wonder if they're not happy with us anymore. I hope you don't mind, but on my way into work today, I started kicking around some ideas. It *might* be a good idea if . . ." Marilyn would have done better by simply saying, "I have a possible solution to the Conant account problem. Could I run some options by you for your opinion?" This method is validated by male workshop participants in surveys taken over the course of ten years: Men want to hear the bottom line.

Almost everyone grows impatient and listens in agony when a person telling a simple story doubles back to give a little piece of background information, rambles on with a little side remark here, and inserts another bit of information there. But men not only feel impatient, they often totally tune out. Marilyn found that the most effective way to reach Dave was to start with the end and then fill in the details as needed. He began to offer ideas and feedback, interacting in the creative process with her instead of spacing out. Short, sweet, and decisive helps.

Be Direct and Specific

Maria operated a manufacturer's representative agency for construction firms. One of the firms hired a man as a regional sales manager for a product. He was always well dressed, but he wore heavy gold accessories and a badly made toupee, and he had an annoyingly aggressive personality. Within a month of taking the line, the new regional sales manager started showing up late for appointments at Maria's office when he came into town. He explained that his tardiness was due to his sexual conquests at bars the night before.

Maria, concerned about the working relationship, tried to hint that she didn't like his being late. She would say, "I'm very busy today," or "Was there a traffic jam?" She would subtly try to steer the conversation in a different direction when he made any comments about his sexual conquests. The subtle approach didn't seem to register with him at all. He showed up almost two hours late for their next appointment. Not surprisingly, the day came when Maria had finally had it. She said, "I don't appreciate it when you show up late at the office, and in the future I'd like a phone call if there is a delay. Also, I would prefer it if you kept your sexual conquests to yourself." Maria made her point crystal clear, and the man never repeated his unprofessional behavior. (Nevertheless, he was extremely fortunate not to lose Maria's account.)

Being direct and specific can also unearth hidden questions or objections during a sale. I (Lee) was making a follow-up call to a potential client regarding a proposed keynote speaker for his association's annual event. I said, "Mr. Harris, I'm following up on our call of three weeks ago when you told me your committee would be meeting last week. What was the interest level for bringing Carolyn Warner in as your keynote speaker?"

Mr. Harris said the committee decided they needed another speaker that could focus on their newly chosen theme, "Community Involvement in Education." I responded, "That's a coincidence. Corwin Press came out last week with Carolyn's new book entitled *Everybody's House—the Schoolhouse: Best Techniques for Connecting Home, School, and Community.*" Harris was surprised: He had not been aware at the time of his committee meeting that Carolyn could speak on that subject. I responded, "Yes, and I believe she would be a good match for your group this year. Let me send you a flyer on the topic so you can present it to your committee." The sale was closed within days. Being specific can pay off.

Make the Interaction a Win-Win Situation

Men are more competitive communicators than women. They look at conversations a little like a game. "Winning points" means getting the last word, the last laugh, the last thought. When you listen to a couple of guys talking, their dialogue may sound like a verbal Ping-Pong match. If a woman is not sensitized to this style difference, she may lose even if she wins. Here is why:

Helene saw Jim, vice president of sales for a medium-sized asphalt paving company, at a chamber of commerce mixer. They had talked the previous month about her sales training services. She walked up to him and asked how business was doing. He embarked on an enthusiastic list of achievements and business opportunities that were obvious ego builders for the image of the company and himself. Helene caught his enthusiasm and related some impressive credentials and recent honors that had been bestowed on her training company. She unwittingly thought that this type of camaraderie would move Jim toward the sale. Instead, Jim redoubled his efforts to win the game by topping Helene with news of some recent high-powered media coverage. Helene then produced an article about her company in a prestigious local newspaper. Suddenly, Helene sensed that she and Jim had a game of one-upsmanship going. Although she felt she was keeping up her end of the competition, she knew she wasn't making the kind of impression that would make the sale.

In this situation, if Helene wins the game, she may lose the sale. She may do better by taking a quietly confident, one-down position and allowing Jim to win the one-up battle so that she can win the war—and make the sale.

Use Humor and Lighten Up

There is nothing that shifts a preconceived notion better than hearty laughter. It is a physical response that opens the possibility for a new point of view. Men instinctively use humor to build rapport with each other, so women in sales must also learn to use humor to build rapport, break tension, and find common ground with men. Take what you do seriously, but don't take yourself too seriously.

What keeps women from being able to lighten up about themselves, their responsibilities, and their colleagues in the workplace? Stress is one major reason. If you are under pressure, laughter is certainly difficult. Because women often feel that they must outperform the guys (remember that Ginger Rogers had to do everything Fred Astaire did, and she had to do it backwards and in high heels), they forget that humor at the appropriate moment is one of the best ways to build rapport with a man.

Maria, the founder of the manufacturer's representative agency, with her partner, Sandy, broke through the gender barrier in the construction industry. They created one of the most prosperous agencies of its kind in the Southwest. They went from zero to $4 million in annual sales in less than six years.

The general manager and national sales manager of a large commercial washroom accessories manufacturer asked to meet with Maria and Sandy. As the interview progressed, the sales manager seemed to be leaning in their favor. He had warmed to their style and was impressed by their solid relationships with Arizona architects. The general manager, however, was visibly squirming in his chair. Finally, he blurted out, "Are there only . . . *gals* in your rep firm?"

They were astounded at the question, but Sandy tossed the ball back into his court with one of her humorous quips: "Well, as a matter of fact, that is correct. However, I have a Great Dane named Hector, a Siamese cat named Freddie, and a parrot named Bud, and they are all guys. But wouldn't you rather work with us?" Within a week they learned that they had made the sale. The reluctant general manager eventually became one of their biggest supporters and took their teasing about his initial attitude with good humor. In fact, he began to repeat the story himself at the annual sales meetings.

Decrease Emotional Intensity

Men and women have different emotional barometers. What a saleswoman might consider appropriate enthusiasm when she is showing a home with a spectacular view may come across as gushy to a man who is interested in the home only as an investment. A woman selling financial services who is trying to seem sincere may come across to a male customer as too emotional. When a saleswoman professes great exuberance for the quality of diamonds she is selling to a male client, her words may come across as exaggerated or phony.

Women in sales need first to lessen the emotions and then build from there. When men are faced with what they see as too much intensity, they can literally withdraw, pull further into themselves, and refuse to disclose their needs or wants. Generally, the more *emotional* the female salesperson becomes, the more *logical* and *rational* the male customer tends to become in response. And when a woman is selling to a man, she needs as much self-disclosure from him as possible.

To open up male customers to your message, first lessen your emotions until you can take his emotional pulse. Observe his body language. Listen to his tone of voice. Note the speed of his speech. Pay attention to his use of feeling words. After lessening your emotions, work up to a sale.

Reprogramming

From the time we are born, we learn from the results of a specific sequence of operations: We cry and we are fed; we walk and are given applause; we get A's in school and receive approval. We tend to repeat the encouraged behaviors and eliminate the ones that are discouraged.

For many centuries women have been encouraged to play a passive role. As Nancy Friday says in her book *My Mother/My Self,* women in prior generations were trained to be someone's "other"—wife, sister, daughter, helpmate. Sales work requires aggressive skills that run counter to much of this early programming. When a younger woman sales professional is bargaining with an older man, her societal role of being a subordinate can potentially undermine the confidence needed to negotiate successfully. Awareness of this situation may be all she needs for a confidence and credibility boost.

When I (Lee) first began my sales career, activities such as cold calls and negotiating were difficult—especially when dealing with high-level male decision-makers over fifty. I experienced sweaty palms, cotton mouth, racing thoughts, and insecurity, which undermined my confidence. By using methods taught to increase the physical performance of athletes, I was able to lessen my emotional state and thereby improve my performance and confidence.

One useful reprogramming technique used by athletes to boost confidence is based on past successes. We often tend to exaggerate the difficulty of a situation while forgetting about past successes and transferable skills. If this sounds familiar, here is a formula you can follow when faced with a high-pressure situation:

1. In the sales challenge at hand, rate your anticipated performance level on a scale of 1 to 10. (You can even put in the dismal figure of -1.)
2. Remember a similar experience where some success was achieved.
3. Rate your performance level for that successful experience on a scale of 1 to 10.
4. Now, rate again your anticipated performance in the sales challenge at hand, on a scale of 1 to 10.

Frequently the result of this exercise is a reduced level of stress, a more realistic picture of the challenge being faced, and a greater likelihood of improved confidence and performance.

Another helpful reprogramming technique focuses on control. The whole idea is to focus your energy only on the aspects of the situation you can actually influence. Follow these steps:

1. List possible obstacles to the successful outcome of a potential sale.
2. Put a "C" beside the factors that you have control over.
3. Put an "NC" beside the factors over which you have no control.

4. Focusing only on the factors you can control, make a list of
   actions you can take to influence the outcome as much as
   possible.

After six months of starting out every day using these reprogramming techniques, my sweaty palms were gone and I had a
more confident approach every time I picked up the phone. For
many women in sales, some reprogramming will counteract the
feeling of being in a "one-down" position. While most salespeople,
men *and* women, have self-imposed limitations, women in particular need to take special notice of potential-limiting messages received from any source.

Many professional women fail to focus on two other crucial areas: risk taking and mentorship. Developing skills in these areas is
important for women influencing men.

Calculate, Then Take Risks

Women in sales need to familiarize themselves with taking risks
when selling to their male customers and must learn to deal with
the fear, uncertainty, and doubt that comes when doing so. Women
have often been programmed to "play it safe," "not make waves,"
and "be nice." Sometimes, however, a sale requires the opposite
behavior.

Information gathering is important in assessing any risk.
Francine, a marketing consultant who knows how to gather information from many sources, said, "If I am going to make a big investment, hire someone, make a change in my business, or sell a
new product, I always do what I call 'taking testimony.' I talk to as
many people as possible—my mother, my children, friends, business associates—and listen to what they have to say. I announce
what I want to do, and I let them all give input. A lot of people
think you have to make decisions in silence, but I think that after

you have talked to twenty people, you have a lot of information. Information is power." And that feeling of power and confidence is the launching pad for risk-taking.

Trish, who sells financial products, agrees with the importance of gathering good information before plunging in. "My methods are very calculated and have proved successful in the past," she said. "On a daily basis I ask myself if I have enough accurate information to make a decision and a good strategic plan. With the right kind of knowledge, I feel better about relying on the less measurable information that comes from intuition and instincts to make my moves."

Sometimes the greatest risk to be faced is taking no risks at all. According to Jacoba, a top producer in the insurance field, "The greatest risk I ever took was to move from the Midwest without a job to come to. To minimize the risk I did my homework and really studied the landscape. There seemed to be a lot of opportunity for someone with my experience, so I quit my job, moved with my four pets, and stayed with my sister for a month. I decided to do whatever it took to make it. The advice I would give to others is 'Go for it.' "

Get a Mentor

Mentoring for women has sometimes been difficult. Often when people find themselves in a minority, they're out of the mentoring and networking loop and don't have access to the "inside" information that gets passed around. They're excluded from the casual passing on of experience, career tips, and other information that happens on the golf course, over a beer, or while playing racquetball.

One male sales professional in the insurance industry commented that women are up against significant resistance from men. The financially successful leaders in the industry are *not* enlightened about women and minority issues. They're comfortable just the way they are and see no reason to share their secrets of success with women who are new to the field. In addition he revealed that there are women in fairly high positions in the insurance industry who may never reach a senior level mainly because they don't have a mentor. Only a person at a very senior management level can invite a woman into the club. Here, men know their roles, who they are, and who likes what; they have activities, clubs, and maybe family connections in common. All of this makes them comfortable with one another. Women need to find someone in that camp who is a good role model and cultivate the relationship so that it becomes a formal or informal mentorship.

Perhaps you can already spot a mentor who would be right for you, or maybe one will emerge during the course of your work. How do you gain someone's confidence or support? You don't have to use the word "mentor." Instead, volunteer to work on a team or project with a person or people you respect. Listen to what they say, observe how they operate, ask intelligent questions when the time is right, and perform in a way that would make experienced people want to work with you again . . . and take you into their fold. Eventually you'll be able to ask your mentor for feedback when you need it or take him or her to lunch for some serious coaching.

Repositioned to Sell

Women are still emerging and climbing the ranks of today's business world, a world where sales is and will be a key growth area for them. Their talents and skills already serve them well; there are plenty of million-dollar female sellers. Even the best of them, though, can always learn something new about the not-always-so-subtle nuances of selling to men. And the best of them are no doubt those who keep learning about the subject.

Understanding the basic precepts of this chapter is the second step toward your future sales success. That's right—the second step. The first step, often overlooked, is continuing to adapt effectively to male communication and buying habits. To thine own self be true, of course. Just develop a willingness to either use or identify with male communication patterns when you need them to make a sale. After all, Gendersell is an action verb, not a way of life.

Repositioning yourself to be the best possible salesperson you can be may also mean dealing with deep-seated doubts and inferiority-complex conditioning, particularly as a woman. At times all of us say or think, "I just can't do it." But this attitude can inhibit some women at a very deep, personal level. The good news is that one can "reprogram" oneself to mask or overcome the difficulties, at least at an operating level, and make definite progress toward becoming an accomplished and confident salesperson.

Practice. That's the bottom line. Practice, practice, practice. Find a colleague or a friend (man or woman) to play the male lead in your sales rehearsals. Work on using the kinds of communication tools and patterns to which men can relate. Self-talk yourself into thinking you can do it, because you can.

And just when you think you're starting to understand how men think and bargain and make purchases, go back and read chapter 3, where men selling to women is discussed—because even though there are many accurate generalizations about men and women, there are many, many variations on the theme. Some male customers may be more sensitive than others, requiring a lighter touch, while some female customers may dumbfound you if you're not quick or direct enough. Adaptability, flexibility, and common sense based on experience will transform you from a good sales professional to a great one.

Chapter 5
Establishing Rapport: Cold and Steely Versus Warm and Fuzzy

She is selling medical transportation services. So is he. She's the salesperson. He is the sales manager. George Heisel and Wendy Springborn-Pitman work for a national private fire and ambulance company, Rural/Metro Corp., which is attempting to keep ahead of the changes in the delivery of health care services. The company's goal is to be a health care transportation resource for nonurgent as well as emergency services. They want to provide transportation for patients' doctor's appointments, for their lab tests, for their outpatient surgery, for all health-related services. They want giant conglomerates of health care delivery systems and small independent hospitals, managed care, and health maintenance organizations to use their services.

The services that George and Wendy are selling are new to most providers and to most consumers. Selling is complex. They have to identify a clear organizational need, determine how their services will save the organization money, find the decision-maker, and persuade him or her to use their as-yet-unproved nonemergency medical transportation services.

Wendy has long been involved in leadership positions in community activities. She lives in a small suburb of a major metropolitan area and knows everybody there is to know: the mayor, the city council members, the environmentalists, the artists, the businesspeople, the cowboys. Her activities range from political action committees to "save the mountains" campaigns. Her name and its association with her company are widely known.

Wendy very indirectly uses her contacts, her reputation as a community activist, and her people skills to schmooze and sell. She acknowledges that she never asks for the business or attempts a hard sell close to the sale. She is very comfortable working with other women, but many of the decision-makers in her industry are men. Wendy worries that her attempts to obtain the business of male customers may be misconstrued as sexual invitations. She has difficulty establishing a comfortable rapport with them early in the game. She finds a slightly flirtatious approach initially works best, but then she doesn't know how to persevere without upping the expectations or without abruptly changing into a business-only mode.

George is new to the company and to the location. He has been involved in selling ambulance services for a longer period of time than Wendy. His approach to selling is direct. He finds out who the decision-maker is and sets out to make an appointment with him or her. He spends lots of time on the telephone, cold-calling the "main man"—the CEO, president, or chief financial officer. He is persistent and pushy. He just keeps on calling. Eventually George will get the CEO on the phone. By then the decision-maker already knows his name because he has received fourteen messages from George. A lunch is set, and George is on his way.

George has a proposal in mind before he even enters the first meeting. He spends a few minutes getting to know the CEO or president and then quickly begins to sell the transportation services his company offers. He opens, presents, and closes at this first meeting. He says he wastes no time "just schmoozing." If the services are declined, George still persists and calls again in one month or three months to have lunch again and talk about changes in the market, the economy, or the offer. Sometimes he has stunning success. Occasionally he has a disaster.

Meanwhile, Wendy is schmoozing away, going to meetings, expanding her network, broadening her knowledge base about people and companies and relationships. In her more indirect manner, she is as persistent as George, at least with female clients. But she is never as pushy. She rarely has the stunning successes that George achieves, but she doesn't have disasters, either.

What Do "Cold" and "Warm" Have to Do with Gender?

Is there only one way to establish rapport with potential clients? If so, which way works best? Clearly, there isn't one right answer. But there are some hypotheses about cold and warm rapport building techniques, about pushy and more passive approaches, about the gender of the salesperson and the gender of the customer, about which method works best under which circumstances.

Although Wendy and George cannot and do not represent all female and all male sales professionals, their styles echo the majority revealed in our research. Wendy has great communication skills and is warm, personable, friendly, outgoing, helpful, sincere, and nurturing. She is definitely an "other-directed" person. George is hard-driving, strategic, a risk taker who will do whatever he has to, within reason and the law, to make the deal. He is pushy, calculating, confident, and independent. He sees these characteristics as a crucial part of his sales success.

Although George and Wendy sell to equal numbers of men and women, they both described their biggest recent success as the result of a long-term relationship-building process with a same-sex client and their biggest disaster with an opposite-sex client. In all likelihood this outcome is not coincidental. The successes and disasters were very much due to the fact that George well knew how to tailor his approach to a man and Wendy well knew how to tailor her approach to a woman. Neither would have been successful with an opposite-sex client unless they had changed their approach. Both of them could have used the Gendersell approach to increase their success rate.

George's Success

George credits his success, in the general sense, to his aggressiveness in seeking out and developing relationships. He thinks that at least in the man's world people like him right off the bat and perceive him as a decision-maker. He earns credibility quickly in the stage of establishing rapport. George values his pushiness. He says, "It's a lot easier to pull back if you're offending someone with your aggressiveness than to finally push ahead when you figure out you've been too passive."

George's most recent success involved landing a big contract that seemed like a definite no. Most of his colleagues thought he would never make the deal even after two years of hard work. His first contact with Lon, the person he called the point man, was a good example of George's strategy. He attended a meeting where Lon was present. Although there was a definite lack of receptivity to George and his company during his first meeting with Lon, George just blew right past it. He started right off by introducing himself before the meeting began and finished off by setting a time to have breakfast alone with Lon—all this despite the fact that (1) George's company already had a conflict-filled history with Lon's facility, (2) George was new to the location, his own company, and the contract, and (3) Lon was decidedly hostile toward George at their first meeting.

Even though the relationship became worse before it became better, even though George had to fight rejection and animosity, even though it would have been much easier to simply give up, George persisted and pushed. He is a patient salesperson and values building a long-term relationship with his clients.

George identified some similarities between himself and Lon. They were from the South, they were Baptists, and they liked baseball. He worked to make those similarities more salient. He determined that what was most important to Lon was his own honesty. George figured that his own and his company's honesty would also be key factors in whether the deal was accomplished. He spent the first year establishing rapport and trust, the second year building the relationship, and the last month selling the deal.

George's Disaster

The disaster for George occurred very early in the rapport-building stage of another sales relationship. His normal pushiness, which usually worked well for him, came across negatively to several women, one of whom was the decision-maker. Interestingly enough, George didn't perceive the event as a disaster but just as a simple mistake.

George had begun cold-calling Rose Wilson, the customer. He introduced himself as the new person in charge of medical transportation services for his company and told her he wanted to meet with her to discuss her facilities' transportation needs. He was direct, straightforward, and to the point. He pressed for an early appointment and got it. When he went to the meeting, he was prepared to do an in-depth needs assessment.

However, Rose wasn't prepared for an intensive data-gathering session. She didn't have all the facts and numbers at her fingertips, and subsequently responded to George's approach with irritation at what she perceived as his aggressive interrogation. When the meeting ended, George was slightly frustrated at not getting the information he wanted as quickly as he wanted it, and Rose was uncomfortable with George's high-pressure tactics.

Their next meeting took place in a public setting where people from other departments in the health care facility, as well as a few other representatives of Rural/Metro Corp., were present. Rose presented some figures about transportation needs, and George said, "Rose, when we met last week, you told me that number was five hundred, not fifty." Rose immediately looked flustered and responded, "No, the number is fifty." George repeated that she had made a mistake. There was one more round of finger-pointing and denial before someone else mercifully changed the focus.

George behaved as he did in most situations: aggressive, confident, a bit challenging, and perhaps even cocky. But in this situation Rose and her female associate perceived his approach as insensitive, degrading, embarrassing, and a put-down. Although Rose never mentioned her reaction to the incident, Greg, an associate of George's also present at the meeting, recognized what was going on.

After the meeting, and with George's okay, Greg took over the sales relationship. He introduced himself after the public meeting and said he would like to meet and follow up with Rose. At the arranged meeting he asked if she had experienced any discomfort with George's style. When Rose responded affirmatively, Greg said that he had noticed her uneasiness and therefore would like to take over the sales relationship if that was agreeable. Rose happily agreed and confessed that she would have been unwilling to continue doing business with George under any circumstances—although she acknowledged that she probably would not have told George directly.

George took the whole experience in stride but didn't necessarily think he could have done it differently. He isn't sure he could start out at a less intense pace even though he understands the importance of relationship-building differences between the genders. With women, George must start building rapport at a much slower pace than he would like. Greg was ultimately successful at winning the business, which happened over a long period of time. The outcome, more than the incident itself, demonstrated to George that he needed to make some changes.

Wendy's Success

Wendy sees herself as straightforward, honest, and reliable, and she believes that others also perceive her that way. She believes that building a relationship is the only key to success. Because she is so active in the community, she almost always knows someone who knows someone who knows someone, and so she never finds herself in the position of making cold calls. She usually connects with people through other people, and she works hard to find real connections, real bonds, real similarities, rather than inventing commonalities. As Wendy says, "What I do is much more than business to me. It is building genuine relationships. I find them and take them as far as they can go." It is much easier for Wendy to build rapport and ultimately establish genuine relationships with women than with men because the line between business and bonding is less likely to become blurred.

Her biggest recent success, not surprisingly, involved two female customers. She had been working on the relationship for two years. The initial connection was made through a mutual acquaintance who knew that Wendy and her potential customer, Joan, were both looking into a weekend MBA program for experienced managers. Wendy's first contact was a genuine information-gathering call. She wanted to pool resources about the program and about similar programs that she had researched.

Joan was delighted and felt comfortable because of the common acquaintance. Eventually they met to talk about their common educational goals and ended up attending the same MBA program, thereby cementing their common bond. This is a classic example of how Wendy prefers to work. She wants to be friends with her customers and wants them to see her as a helpful partner. She would hate to be viewed as aggressive or insincere. She says, "I just can't toot my own horn. I don't want to, and I don't want people to see me as that kind of person."

Wendy's Fade

Interestingly, Wendy hasn't had any disasters. In contrast to George, who could immediately identify more than one, Wendy had trouble coming up with any. Is it because she is in denial and doesn't know her own shortcomings? Probably not. Wendy speculated that her nurturing approach rarely leads to catastrophe. The deal slips away or just doesn't happen, and Wendy isn't sure quite why. Is it because she can't partner as well with men? Is it because with some customers she is not pushy enough? Is it due to the fact that she never gets to the relationship-building stage with men? Do they see her as unknowledgeable? Or do her relationships with men never get to the point where credibility is an issue? Does she ever really get direct and ask for the business?

Wendy is not sure, but she feels strongly that she is at her best when working with women and operating in the style that is hers. She thinks that changing would be almost impossible. She doesn't want to sell in a different way even if that would mean working more effectively with some of her male customers. If Wendy needs to close more sales in general, and create rapport with more male clients in particular, she'll have to make some significant changes.

Gendersell Generalities

Rapport refers to the connection, agreement, and harmony between people. We think of it as the quick presence of positive, nonsexual chemistry between people. Because perceived similarity is the quickest route to instant rapport, each gender may be more naturally comfortable with its own. Therefore, if there is no positive chemistry but only a neutral feeling between people, the salesperson will be required to exert effort in order for rapport to be achieved.

Tips for Building Rapport with Women

Since George's target market—high-level decision-makers in the health care industry—is rapidly shifting from almost all men to a fifty-fifty split, he is going to have to adapt to working with women—and so are most of the men sales professionals reading this book. Regardless of your field or industry, as a man in sales your customer base is probably changing. You, too, will need to fine-tune your skills.

Go Slowly

In setting up his first meeting with Rose, George might have taken what we call a strong one-down position. It is strong because you choose it instead of accepting it by default. It's a one-down position because you have decided that a one-up position won't work in the situation. You purposely avoid the perception of aggressiveness or a win-lose situation by choosing to seem collaborative instead of competitive. In order to achieve this, you'll need a different set of verbal and nonverbal behaviors. But this doesn't mean you can't still be an aggressive salesman internally; you just can't act that way externally.

In the rapport-building stage, the only item on the agenda of your first brief meeting may be getting to know your female customer. You also need to give her an opportunity to get to know you personally and professionally. This is a good time to get some information about just how slow or fast you should proceed from this point on. Maybe you'll determine that once she gets to know you, she'll be ready to push through with the sale.

Rapport doesn't happen in two minutes. We know that rapport is generally more important to women than to men. We know that collaboration rather than competition is more admired by women than by men. So here is the opportunity to put this knowledge into practice. While you are going slow, which may seem tedious at times and against your basic nature, you may need to remind yourself to accept the fact that, as customers, women are higher maintenance than men. But a deal is a deal, a sale is a sale, and since women will continue to gain power in all types of organizations, adapting is a necessity.

Act in Accord

In the rapport-building phase of the sales relationship, acquiring trust is essential, particularly with women. Acting in accord is a powerful way to demonstrate that you take the female customer seriously, that you see her as knowledgeable, credible, and powerful. "Acting in accord" means behaving as if what the customer is saying is *true for her.* How? Simply affirm and believe what the customer is saying rather than probing, interrogating, challenging, disputing, or arguing. For example, if a client says, "I don't want to have high ceilings in my new house. It's too ostentatious a look for me," you would act in *discord* by saying, "Everyone loves these high ceilings once they get used to them. They're not ostentatious; they just create an elegant environment." Acting in accord or harmony would be to say, "I'd like to show you one other model that has high ceilings. It doesn't seem ostentatious to me, but I'd like your opinion on it. I may be wrong. Then we'll stop looking at high-ceilinged houses."

The scenario with George and Rose would have been far more successful if George had *privately* clarified the numbers with Rose and had taken responsibility for the confusion. For example, "Rose, you just mentioned that you had fifty trips a month. I must have misunderstood the first time we spoke about this because I wrote down five hundred. Fifty is the right number, then?" That is acting in accord.

The fact that many men find it difficult to admit fault is recognized by men themselves. An occasional genuine "I'm sorry" or acknowledging that your information may not have been accurate would be acting in accord with a female customer. While this technique may not work with male customers, acting in accord could boost your performance. (A "gender joke" says that in personal relationships, contrary to popular opinion, the three little words that women want to hear from men are *not* "I love you" but "I was wrong.")

Men often think women are too quick to take offense and are sometimes hypersensitive or even paranoid. Men also state that women read too much into what men say or do. The reality is that women *are* generally more reactive than men to perceived slights or challenges, criticisms or put-downs. Again, the difference isn't right or wrong, it just is, so as a male sales professional you should simply take it into account and adjust for it by trying to act in accord.

Tips for Building Rapport with Men

Wendy has a surefire way of building rapport with women. Although she has difficulty making the transition from the "establishing a relationship" mode to the "closing" mode with women, she at least gets there. With men, Wendy seems unable to even get through the building-rapport phase of establishing a relationship. Although she doesn't experience disasters because of this lack, she doesn't make the quantity or quality of sales that she could if she dealt more effectively with male customers early on. Let's look at some ways that sales professionals can improve their rapport with men.

Reprogramming

There is no doubt about it: For many female sales professionals, reprogramming is essential to becoming more adaptive.

There are three steps in reprogramming. The first step is to decide that you want to increase your sales to men. Then you need to rethink and restructure your identity vis-à-vis men. Many women rely on old roles and rules, and, like Wendy, find themselves somewhat uncertain. Does your usual sales stance make you seem subservient or a lightweight? If you are naturally flirtatious, are you taken seriously or considered a sex object? If you are aggressive, will you turn off your male customers?

The second step is to reformat your role in your own mind. How can you think differently about yourself as a sales professional working with male customers? Perhaps the best way is to think of yourself as someone selling services that are desperately needed. Wendy has no trouble selling her ideas about saving mountain preserves, because she thinks her ideas truly benefit the community. If she can begin to think that the transportation services she is selling are as beneficial to clients as saving land is to the community, she might be able to be more aggressive in influencing male and female clients. Rehearsing the new role with a friend or colleague is a useful way to move from adaptive thinking to adaptive behavior with a client.

The third step is changing your internal dialogue. Whether you really believe it or not, you need to tell yourself that you *can* do it. Thinking positively doesn't necessarily work, but *not* thinking negatively always helps. Neutral and instructional internal monologues work best, so instead of negatively thinking "I'm not sure how to handle this" or "I never work well with macho males" or "I must be coming across as just plain stupid or silly," you need to think: "I'm making some changes that will help." "One step at a time, and I can improve my skills with male customers." "This is going to be fun and educational for me." "What do I have to lose? What

I'm doing isn't working, so I might as well try something new. The worst thing that can happen is that it won't work, either."

Get a Mentor

Generally, women learn well from other people. Finding a female sales professional to serve as a good role model in the area of establishing rapport with men would be helpful to Wendy as well as to many women in sales. Someone who comes across professionally without seeming either pushy or flirtatious would be an appropriate person to emulate. You might also be able to change your mind-set about yourself as a salesperson by connecting to another woman you admire who is very much a salesperson and proud of it. A female mentor could also tell you how she overcame obstacles similar to those you're experiencing, and she can inspire you to keep on trying new approaches to the problem.

Take a Confident Tone

Wendy needs to build credibility as a salesperson with her customers as well as herself. She doesn't have to work so hard at product knowledge of her company's transportation services because she never even gets to that point with the male customer. In the early rapport-establishment stage, she has to come across as a business representative of her company, rather than a social representative of her gender or her community.

By doing a good job putting herself in business professional mode—which includes talking knowledgeably about the business, the customers' business, and the industry in general—Wendy can set the stage for the close later. A minimum of conversation about her personal life is best. The only time to talk about family or interests is if it adds to the customer's perception of similarity. With male customers Wendy will also decrease the likelihood of awkwardness or confusion about the nature of the relationship by sticking to business. A more confident tone and approach will further solidify the business relationship.

Get to the Point Early or Speed Up the Sales Pitch

It is important for Wendy to realize that the rapport-building stage may not take as long with men as it does with women. The sooner she clearly states what she does, what she wants, and what she sees in it for the male customer, the sooner she can clarify respective roles and erase any potentially unrealistic expectations. That doesn't mean Wendy can't use her outgoing personality as a catalyst to doing business, but it does mean that she should make the transition quickly into sales mode.

Many women are concerned that people will think they are pushy and using a hard sell. Instead they should realize that men want women to get to the point more quickly. They will then be able to see that this mode of behavior pleases people and doesn't appear pushy.

What to Do Differently to Establish Rapport with the Opposite Sex

The rapport-building stage is obviously essential. No rapport, no nothing. As a sales professional you might calculate what percentage of your initial contacts with customers of the opposite sex were successful. Then aim to increase that percentage in the first month of Gendersell practice.

Women should work at

• setting a clear goal to increase their effectiveness in selling to men;
• establishing their role as a business partner early in the contact by looking, sounding, and acting the part;
• finding an experienced female mentor who is willing to help them find and define the line between too female and too male, too tough and too tender; this mentor should model, teach, and inspire;
• keeping all conversations related to business or their male clients' interests, leaving out their own stuff;
• moving more quickly toward the presentation or close than they would with a female customer.

Men should work at

• taking a deep breath or two and slowing down the pace;
• being more formal and polite rather than less; using the customer's name rather than informal expressions such as dear or hon. The word "women" should be used to describe groups of female people;
• spending time and energy getting to know their female customers so they will be interested in continuing the relationship.
• talking about her, her business, her interests, and her needs, and not about themselves;
• hearing what she says and recognizing that it is true for her, and not challenging, arguing, or disputing her opinions unless she conveys total misinformation about the product she is purchasing.

Chapter 6
Building and Bonding
the Customer Connection

Stephen Barnes is a Chartered Financial Analyst. Kathie, his wife, is a Certified Financial Planner. Their company, Barnes Investment Advisory, provides financial advice and investment management to an equal number of individuals and couples. They have been extremely successful at what they do, as indicated by their recognition in *Worth* magazine as one of the top two hundred financial planning companies in the United States. Their achievement is especially notable when you consider that they are both in their late thirties.

Kathie and Stephen have worked in the field of finance for fourteen years. They merged their separate businesses about eight years ago, and they see themselves very much as a team. As you will see, their conviction about teamwork is much less a philosophical choice than a practical necessity. Neither one of them can or wants to do all the tasks, and neither has all the skills necessary to run the show. So they have chosen to rely on each other to fill in the gaps.

When you meet Kathie and Stephen, they don't really look as if they go together. He is dark-haired and slim, sort of bookish looking without glasses. He is not quick to smile and comes across as a bit aloof, although not unfriendly. When you are with Stephen, he seems to be thinking about far-off financial figures instead of the immediate conversation. Kathie, on the other hand, is warm, smiling, and friendly, although not at all gushing. She leans forward in her chair when talking to you and nods her head as you talk. She is very clearly there with you at every turn of the conversation. She is blond and pretty, rounder rather than angular, vivid rather than somber.

These differences between Kathie and Stephen are fairly typical in terms of gender. George and Wendy, discussed in the last chapter, could be described similarly to Stephen and Kathie: relative seriousness, distance, and coolness on the part of the men, and colorfulness, warmth, and closeness on the part of the women.

Kathie and Stephen work together with clients in different ways, depending on the client request, the referral source, the anticipated client needs, and the client's personality. If a client requests an appointment with Stephen, she will eventually be introduced to Kathie—usually by the first or second meeting. When a client who mainly needs investment advice is referred to Kathie, she usually brings Stephen to the first meeting as the co-owner of the business and the primary investment manager. Otherwise, she'll wait a bit and see how things work out.

Kathie generally makes the final decisions about which of them will work with which client. She also determines when, where, and how much the other will be brought into the relationship. Kathie is particularly good at sensing when a client would do better with less of Stephen and more of her, and vice versa. They both agree that she is much better at reading, interviewing, and assessing people, and both recognize that seeing all clients at all stages of the process isn't cost or talent effective.

Kathie and Stephen would like to have a reliable system that their secretary could use to assign each adviser to a specific client, but in practice they have found that working on a case-by-case basis is best in terms of client satisfaction.

What Does Bonding Have to Do with Selling?

What makes certain people like or dislike others? Do customers have to like salespeople in order to do business with them? Once you have successfully established rapport with your customer, can you decide that the tough part is over and relax a bit? After rapport exists, is product knowledge the key?

Similarity is certainly a factor in building relationships. When your customer is very different from you, finding something in common may be difficult. But when you start to move from establishing rapport to building a relationship with a customer, commonalities aren't enough. More has to happen—ideally, that the customer likes you as a salesperson. When people act as if they like us, we tend to think they are people of good judgment, discerning taste, and perceptiveness. As customers we act friendlier, open up a bit more, and want to spend time with, instead of avoid, the salesperson.

The female customer has to see you not only as someone who knows what he is talking about but also as someone who has a true, genuine interest in her well-being. The customer wants a business friend, an ally, a partner. In situations that ideally will continue over time—for example, a financial, legal, or medical services relationship, or a relationship with a jeweler, dry cleaner, or business equipment salesperson—more than rapport must be established. Women as customers are often more concerned about the "liking" factor than men.

A Phoenix family-run business, Schmitt's Jewelers, has done an outstanding job of establishing long-term relationships with their customers. Both the older and younger generations remember and comment about the customer's family and special occasions. "Isn't Sara about to graduate from college?" they say in January when you're in the store for a watch repair. When the customer—

pleasantly pleased at the comment and surprised because she hadn't even begun to think about a gift for Sara—confirms the fact, the response is "When you have time, come on back. We have some great ideas for graduation gifts this year. And we have some new amethyst jewelry in if you'd like to think of that for her birthday in February." The customer is stunned but doesn't feel the least bit pressured because the comments seem genuine and caring. The jewelers seem to like not only the customer but also the entire family. This is what bonding and building a relationship has to do with selling. This is what Kathie and Stephen have to do as well.

Stephen's Strengths and Weaknesses

Stephen's strength is looking and acting like an expert. He is confident and credible. This credibility is based on his completion of various certification programs as well as the Certified Financial Analyst program, which carries great weight with financial advisers. He has been active in the CFA Society and has made some terrific contacts. Many have given him good media exposure and frequent referrals. Perhaps some stereotypes about men and money have helped, but Stephen has ended up as a financial guru—smart, wise, inscrutable, and cerebral.

What about his bonding abilities? Although smart, he still has to come across as accessible and trustworthy. He still has to be able to build rapport and move on to establishing a long-term relationship. Women in particular want to think he is a caring kind of guy who's interested in more than number crunching—at least if they are going to allow *him* to invest their money.

One of the most difficult situations Stephen encountered was with a female client who thought he did not understand her needs adequately. She felt misunderstood and took her business elsewhere because of what she perceived as Stephen's lack of people skills. He focused on the numbers and the business. "I'm convinced this investment is the best possible use of your money at this time. The company has been in business for many years. Their future is solid. Their history is untarnished. The analysts consistently support them. You can count on 12 percent a year." She wanted instead: "I think this investment will provide the comfort and stability that you need in the next five years or so. With so many changes coming up in your life, you need a solid, reliable, hassle-free way to be certain that your money will be making money." Maybe no one could have given this client what she wanted or needed, but Stephen thinks he could have done better with building that relationship.

Stephen readily acknowledges that he wouldn't be successful in business if Kathie didn't have the relationship skills that he lacks. He knows he needs to do better in that area. He has tried to do better, he wants to do better, but he finds the skills that Kathie has are amazingly difficult to acquire.

Kathie's Strengths and Weaknesses

Kathie's strength is in her ability to connect with people. She is the builder and bonder. She remembers people's names and their family members' names. She knows which child plays soccer and which plays basketball. She asks about ailing parents and new puppies. She inquires about vacations and new home purchases. The clients love her.

As with Stephen's financial acumen, Kathie views this facility with clients as a natural ability. She doesn't have to work hard in order to come across as interested and real. She genuinely cares, so she tends to remember information about clients' families and life events.

Although both Kathie and Stephen value Kathie's ability to build relationships and agree that they never could have achieved success without them, there is still the subtle implication that somehow this skill is less valuable than expert knowledge. Though Kathie does have financial knowledge, keeping it at her fingertips in detailed, quantitative form is as difficult for her as remembering clients' children's names is for Stephen. Another difference here is that while Stephen wants and thinks he has to get better at relationship-building skills, Kathie doesn't particularly want to increase her number-crunching skills or spend more time on additional certifications. Nevertheless, she harbors a slight insecurity from being seen as the lightweight on the team.

When things have not gone well for Kathie, the problem seems to stem from her perceived lack of credibility in the financial arena. Although her clients have said that she didn't give them the right information, timely information, or good advice, she thinks that the problem has to do with her failure to build an important stage of the relationship.

Gendersell Generalities

Remember that, generally, women are more interested in people, feelings, and relationships, and men are more interested in business, money, and sports. It is not surprising, therefore, that Kathie likes the relationship-building process more than Stephen does, and Stephen likes the quantitative, analytical thinking, planning, and discussion more than Kathie does.

Although relationship-building skills have historically not been valued as much as quantitative, technical, or leadership skills in management, or product knowledge in sales, the pendulum is swinging. Shelly Lazarus is credited with being well able to cultivate and maintain personal relationships with a broad spectrum of people, including employees and clients. Although there has been criticism, perhaps from traditionalists, that her success has been due less to substance than to sociability, she nevertheless was recently promoted to CEO of Ogilvy and Mather Worldwide, one of the biggest advertising agencies in New York.

For female customers as well as female sales professionals, the *how* of selling is equal to or more important than the *what* of selling. As Faith Popcorn points out in her book *Clicking,* women make connections everywhere they go. Connecting defines the way women relate to the business world and how they will change the world. Popcorn talks about FemaleThink as NewThink. In our view, Gendersell is a perfect example of NewThink.

Establishing rapport is a critical first step, but it is only a first step. For many women, if rapport doesn't lead to bonding or the bonding doesn't build, the deal is off. A recent experience demonstrates the point well. Lee and I were shopping for an attorney who specialized in publishing—a person not easy to come by in Phoenix, Arizona. Finally, through a longtime female friend in New York, we found a man who had experience with publishing and with professional speakers. We were delighted.

Our first meeting went well. He was warm, funny, knowledgeable, and confident. He was sort of "showbiz," and he dropped names like Tony Robbins and John Gray. He asked a lot of questions and took notes. He told us he knew people in the publishing business he could check with, at no additional cost to us, and he would get back to us within the week. We were excited and relieved. Here was someone we could lean on for his expertise. He could be our lawyer for all future ventures, joint or separate. He understood the world of rights, which seemed overwhelming to us. He was interested, not patronizing, and clearly knowledgeable. Rapport was definitely there.

No call came from him within the week. The next week, when we called and suggested a meeting, he agreed. But this time he was a different person. He clearly was squeezing us into his busy schedule. He was running late. He had no notes in front of him and almost no recollection of our conversation. What he remembered was incorrect.

The outcome? We didn't build a relationship. We didn't bond. And we did not return to his office again. Men may have found him equally as inadequate, but they would have been less likely to exit as quickly or completely. Perhaps we seem overly critical and demanding. Perhaps many female customers seem that way to many men and women in sales. But women want to connect. They connect when the sales professional remembers their concerns and needs, pays attention, seems to listen, and values their business.

Kathie and Stephen's business, financial products and services, is still largely male in terms of culture. The industry has been slow to recognize and pursue the huge untapped market of women who have money to invest and retirements to plan for.

In an article in the *Dow Jones Investment Advisor,* writer Olivia Mellan identifies major gender differences in attitudes toward money, which she says affect how the sexes want to work with financial advisers. Women are more cautious, more open to advice, and less comfortable with financial risk than men. Men are more confident in their own knowledge and experience, less risk aversive, and have more ego involvement than women investors. Because of these differences, learning how to educate, advise, and sell specifically to men and women has become a necessity.

What Is a Better Way to Connect with Women?

Stephen doesn't have a big need to change right now because he has a partner who can do what he can't do. Nonetheless, he recognizes that he is taking a big risk by not working on his relationship-building skills, particularly with women. The same is true for other men in sales whose strengths may be their experience, in-depth understanding of their product, and a solid customer base of men. Connecting through communication and relationship skills rather than solely through product knowledge and industry credibility works.

Build a Relationship

Although Stephen has said he has tried to improve at the early stages of the sales process, he hasn't set up the kind of definitive plan he might create if he were determined to learn Spanish or golf. Men in sales need to make learning people skills a high priority if they want to be effective when selling to women. Stephen might work on connecting better by meeting weekly with Kathie and a new female customer or couple for the initial interview. He can alternate between watching how Kathie connects, adapting his approach, and having her critique his people skills. For men in sales who aren't strong in relationship building, working with women in a team approach is a good way to learn and improve.

Listening and Asking—Not Telling

After observing Kathie, Stephen can focus on really listening and asking questions instead of telling. He may take notes if it will improve his ability to listen and retain. Instead of honing in quickly on the financial landscape, he can spend a significant amount of time asking the female customer or couple about their goals, their history, their current interests, their work, their family. He can respond with active listening techniques instead of questions that sound like interrogations. For example, "Sounds as if your family's educational needs are a high priority right now" is better than "Exactly how much money do you think you're going to need in the next five years to take care of the family's educational needs?" Confirming queries by saying, "Then what is of greatest concern to you both is the security of knowing you are prepared to deal with any unexpected financial demands," is better than "Is security the most important motivating force for you both?"

Stephen can increase his eye contact and head nodding, and flash an occasional smile. At this stage being accessible, not intimidating, is most important. There is plenty of time to be the expert later. He can ask some "irrelevant" questions: What are your children's names? What are your son's interests? Where is your daughter thinking of going to college?

Meantime, Kathie can take a somewhat secondary role—not a passive, one-down position, just a less active one. She can establish her own relationship at the same time but give Stephen more of the time to be the schmoozer. After the meeting they can sit down for fifteen or twenty minutes to critique Stephen's performance. Did he come across as warm and accessible? Did he make eye contact, smile occasionally, maybe even use a little humor? Did he paraphrase and reflect the feeling of the female client? And, most important, what did he learn that will be useful in continuing to build the relationship? Did he notice anything in particular about the customer's needs, expressed or not? Can he remember the children's names and one fact about them? Does he have some thoughts he can write down now about how to start the conversation the next time he talks with the customer? Do his hypotheses match Kathie's? If not, can they figure out where their different perceptions come from? Can they agree to agree or agree to disagree? Can they plan the next step in the bonding process for Stephen?

Increase the Use of Feeling Words and Emotional Events

The good news for Stephen is that he doesn't have to turn into an expressive, sensitive, emotional kind of guy. All he needs to do is increase slightly the emotional intensity of his conversation with female clients. What that means is that he should be a little more outgoing, a little more friendly, a little warmer. It also means he should use more feeling words and relate his quantitative, logical information to emotional events more frequently.

Stephen can use the feeling words when he is talking about himself as well as when he is talking about his clients. No, he doesn't have to say, "I'm thrilled to have you as a client," but he can say, "I'm pleased that you chose us as your financial advisers. I'm enthusiastic about our working together to build the outcomes that you want." When he is talking about his clients, he can occasionally use feeling words when summarizing his impressions: "I noted how committed you both are about educating your children well." "I sensed that you are both excited about embarking on a new investment strategy." Or he can give his female client a "twofer": his feelings and her feelings. "I'm impressed with your determination to complete your estate planning in the next three months. I'll match your enthusiasm and dedication so we'll be sure to meet your goal." These kinds of "feeling" words don't have to fill every sentence. A few feeling words are sufficient in every client conversation that last more than five minutes. Some low-key positive feeling words that men might feel comfortable using:

- confident
- pleased
- comfortable
- certain
- enthusiastic
- excited

Some low-key negative feeling words that men might feel comfortable using:

- uncertain
- concerned
- uncomfortable
- bothered
- restrained
- cautious

Including emotional events in the conversation is another way to come across as more accessible. Stephen could say: "It's easy for me to remember your birthday because it's the same as my sister's." "I can guess that planning for your daughter's graduation is probably diverting your attention from some of this nuts-and-bolts money stuff at the moment." "Retirement is a complex concept. It has different meanings for different people. What are your thoughts now about your future retirement?" As with feeling words, emotional events don't have to be liberally strewn throughout every conversation, just occasionally sprinkled in.

Better Relationship Building with Men

Kathie still needs to work on ways to build credibility so that if she needs to be seen as an expert, she doesn't have to start at ground zero. She has the product knowledge; she just has to *come across* as an expert. Although she doesn't want or need to be in competition with Stephen, Kathie needs to know that she can come across as an expert in money matters whenever she wants. Here is how.

Build Credibility

What is the best way to showcase Kathie's product knowledge? As Stephen improves his relationship-building skills, Kathie can feel less responsibility for being the bonder-builder-schmoozer at all times. This will allow her more time to focus on money matters. Because people form impressions quickly and because societal stereotypes will lead many people to think of Kathie as the financial lightweight of the pair, an early indication of her expertise will be needed with new clients.

The first way she can promote herself is in introductions to clients. Like many women, Kathie has some difficulty tooting her own horn. She doesn't have to be boastfully obnoxious, but telling people briefly, concisely, and matter-of-factly about her background, her experience, her certifications, her professional associations, and her expert status as a radio host for a financial advice program will work wonders. Male clients like to know specific credentials, particularly when a woman works in a traditionally male field or industry. Men are used to hearing statistics; they are not put off unless the approach is based on style and emotion rather than on substance and logic. "I'm the best in the business and worth every cent that you'll pay me for my services" doesn't build credibility with men. "I've been in the financial services field for thirteen years and have been owner of my own business for eight years" does.

Jill Barad, CEO of Mattel, has acknowledged that because she wasn't able to network with men in the "usual" way, she compensated by always making herself visible. Undoubtedly there were colleagues along the way who found her determination and pursuit of visibility unattractive or even negative. However, she probably wouldn't have arrived at her current position if she hadn't focused on promoting herself.

Female clients or customers can respond negatively to female sales professionals who toot their own horn too loudly. Because they may buy into some traditional beliefs about modesty in women or see credential-waving as bragging, they may view other sales professionals' efforts to build credibility as tacky self-promotion. When women are selling to men and women, a solid presentation of credentials is needed. Even if female clients may be put off to begin with, the female sales professional can often get them back later with her relationship skills. On the other hand, if she doesn't build credibility with the men, she has lost them forever.

Occasionally Kathie may need to take the head-of-the-table or behind-the-big-desk position to increase her visibility and, consequently, the perception that she and Stephen are on equal footing when it comes to their knowledge base. Her office and the conference room should both have liberal displays of awards, plaques, licenses, and certificates related to her accomplishments.

Although both Kathie and Stephen agree that Stephen is better at answering questions and at thinking on his feet financially, Kathie can still attach herself to the charts, financial analyses, and graphs that both have put together. Taking a slightly bigger role in this aspect of early selling would certainly increase client confidence and comfort with her knowledge.

Use Business, Money, and Sports Terminology

In the same way that men can use feeling words to their advantage, women can artfully use words and references that will interest men. Although this advice is good across the board, it is even more fitting in the financial sector. Occasional name-dropping always works. Kathie could say, "I noticed in *The Wall Street Journal* this morning . . ." or "When I was reading *Fortune* last week . . ." or "There was an interesting article in *Forbes* that I thought you'd like. It fits your situation to a T."

The ability to know what is going on in local business is important. Is there a new bank coming to town? A new developer building homes? A noteworthy merger or acquisition? A change in the local economy or political climate? Most men are tuned in to these events and perceive a woman who is equally informed as knowledgeable—and, even better, similar to them.

Keeping attuned to the sports world is always an asset to women in business. In major American cities, teams are the binding force that tie many people to the community. Knowing what is going on locally and nationally—at least on a conversational level—is another essential way of building credibility with men. For Kathie, being able to use sports metaphors to illustrate a financial point would bolster her image. Kathie might say, "The Suns had to make a choice. They could choose speed or strength or size in their draft pick, but they couldn't get all three assets in the same person. In your investment strategy, you have to make a choice, too. You can choose growth or income. You can choose high or low risk. You can choose a lot of personal control or not much personal control. But like the Suns, you probably can't get all your choices in one investment strategy."

Kathie can also gain credibility by talking about computers, a topic that she knows well. As a recent *Wall Street Journal* headline announced, "Forget Cars, Sports or Sex: Guys Today Want to Talk PCs." Although Kathie is actually a "computer nerd" of sorts, she just hasn't had the same compulsion to talk about the subject as many men do. But some solid evidence of software and hardware expertise would give Kathie a boost up the authority ladder.

Because our research revealed that women tend to prefer to receive financial advice from men, Kathie will perhaps increase her credibility with both female and male customers if she sometimes communicates more like a man.

What You Can Do Differently to Build Your Relationship with the Opposite Sex

The relationship-building stage continues throughout and beyond the actual close of a sale. Bonding is a continuous process, and you can damage or even lose the relationship at any stage in selling. And when that happens, you can lose the sale.

For men, putting in the effort at this stage will pay off in the long run. Here are some surefire ways to bond with a female client:

- Set a goal to improve your performance in this stage of selling.
- Think of success as establishing a relationship, not making the sale.
- Take the female customer seriously: Listen, ask, maintain eye contact, remember what she said, assume she's intelligent.
- Talk more emotionally than you would with men; use some feeling words, refer to events, transitions, and life experiences that are associated with strong sentiments.

For women, establishing credibility as a product expert at this stage will make the rest of the sales process go more quickly and smoothly. Here are some ways:

- Start out by giving your credentials—whether it is years of experience, academic background, advanced training, or passion for the product. Look and act like an expert even if you don't feel it.
- Particularly if you're in a male-dominated business, be ultra-concise and knowledgeable about the specific product or service and about the industry in general.
- Be sure to take the opportunity to refer to business, sports, and the economy in order to demonstrate your similarity to your male clients.

Chapter 7
Finding a Fit—the Needs Assessment by Gender

The needs assessment is unique in sales because it is the only stage of selling where you and the customer are doing exactly the same thing. Although customers aren't usually working on establishing relationships, doing presentations, or closing the sale, they are trying to find a fit. The dynamic nature of the two-way assessment adds to the complexity of a process that is already fluid due to new products, services, and markets.

Potential purchasers have a need to fill or a problem to solve, which is why they are looking to buy your product or service. The need may be obvious and stated clearly and directly: A single male may have adopted a baby and has a one-bedroom house. He needs a bigger house. That is pretty straightforward. However, some situations are more ambiguous. The purchaser may know his real need but not want you to know. He may want to live in a neighborhood where a gay single man with a baby will find acceptance or at least not be bombarded with rejection—but he may not want to tell the salesperson that concern.

In many circumstances the client is not sure what problem he is trying to solve. Customers may not know their underlying motivation to buy a new computer, a printing franchise, a piece of sculpture, a series of cooking lessons, a health club membership. Maybe he is buying a new boat to divert his attention from the fact that he didn't get the job promotion he expected. Or perhaps she is buying a small office building to prove her independence and demonstrate her financial strength to her former husband.

Ambiguous scenarios like these sometimes make it necessary for the sales professional to take on the role of both mind reader and therapist. When you and your client are somewhat similar, the psychologist role is easier. When you and your client are of the opposite sex, picking up on motivation and needs is far more difficult. "What do women want?" and "What makes guys tick?" are common questions that every man and woman wants to know. The answers are critical to the sales professional.

In his book *The 7 Habits of Highly Effective People,* Stephen Covey asserts that the single most important principle to internalize is "Seek to understand, then to be understood." Seeking to understand is also the primary goal of any type of needs assessment. Until sales professionals truly understand their customers, they can't possibly determine if their product fits the customer's needs. Although each step in the sales process has its own significance, conducting a good needs assessment may be the most important stage of all if you're selling high-end and/or complex products or services and want the client to be a customer for life.

Seek first to understand. We have a tendency to assume that what works for us will work for others; what we like, our customers will like; what meets our needs will meet theirs. The famous golden rule—Do unto others as you would have done unto you—creates great outcomes when you and your customer are similar. When you're not, the platinum rule is more effective: Do unto others as they would have done unto them. This is the crux of the Gendersell approach.

A residential realtor friend says she has given up assuming anything about client needs. When taking a couple through the kitchen of a potential new home, she always asks who does the cooking for the family. She has heard a variety of answers: "We have a live-in cook." "We don't cook at all, so we don't really need a kitchen." "I'm a househusband and a gourmet cook."

While walking in the customer's shoes—looking at the purchase from her point of view or seeing how your product or service fits with his lifestyle—isn't easy, it is needed now more than ever. Men and women will continue to be different. Roles and rules will change daily. Niche markets will be refined and redefined. Assuming difference rather than similarity is a more effective strategy for selling today. Yes, you should look for similarities that can help you establish rapport, but seeing the differences early and clearly will help you do a better job of diagnosis.

Gendersell Generalities

Research on gender similarities and differences shows that women are better than men at reading people. In particular, they are good at figuring out the meaning of nonverbal behavior and the nature of underlying emotions. This doesn't mean that men can't acquire the same level of skill in reading customers' needs and motivations, but that learning will take concerted effort.

In addition, women in sales often proceed more slowly than men, so they have more time during the rapport-establishment and relationship-building phases to gather information and think about client needs. Our survey respondents also indicated that they perceive women in sales as adept at determining customer needs and fitting a product or service to those needs rather than forcing a customer to adapt to an available product.

Can men do a good job at this step in the sales process? Of course. Jay Chalmers, vice president of marketing for The Executive Committee (TEC), identifies his greatest strength as asking a narrowly targeted stream of highly focused questions to determine if client needs can or cannot be met through TEC membership. TEC is an international organization of CEOs who are leaders of businesses with more than twenty-five employees and more than $3 million in annual sales. The organization prides itself on selecting only members who will benefit from and be beneficial to the membership. Consequently, a very specific form of needs assessment, which TEC calls the selection interview, is critical.

Jay thinks that women's advantage in the selection interview is that both female and male clients are often more open with women than with men. Male clients may also enjoy the sexual attraction potential of talking openly and sometimes personally with women. Men talking with men are often dealing with competition issues, which may keep them from revealing problems or inadequacies as business leaders. On the other hand, many women—even very successful business owners—are concerned that they'll be judged inadequate by men's standards or that their different way of doing things will be deemed a violation of "the rules of the game." This attitude can lead to greater comfort when dialoguing with women.

Jay commented that his biggest surprise, when TEC started recruiting more women as chairs of groups of CEOs, was that women were not any better than men at dealing with the emotional aspects of the selection interview. Both sexes assiduously avoid the feeling words when they're doing an assessment interview. A potential client might say, "I'm worried about my plant manager's ability to do his job." Rather than homing in on the emotion—"Tell me more about your concern"—most of the interviewers say something that moves them quickly away from the feelings: "What's your plant manager's name? How long has he been working for you? Exactly what is his job?" Jay sees this general avoidance of the feeling component as a major obstacle to coming up with a good selection fit.

John and Colleen Gyori, who sell residential real estate as partners for Executive Realty, see tremendous gender differences in each other as salespeople. Like the financial planners Stephen and Kathie in the last chapter, they agree that Colleen is far superior to John in determining client needs and finding and fitting a house to their needs. She is so confident in her ability that she has been known to tell her husband, "I've found the house that the Robinsons are going to buy." This conversation takes place *before* the Robinsons have seen or even heard about the house she has found for them. And as John affirms, Colleen is almost always right.

Colleen goes so far as to say, "I'm not a salesperson personality. I'm just good at getting people to tell me their needs. I listen. I get into my clients' heads. I figure out what they really want, even if they don't always know." She and John both see the home-buying process as very emotional for their clients. Both feel that they deal well with the high levels of emotion involved in the sales process. Colleen has trouble when emotions aren't involved because she has a harder time reading them. In contrast, John says he does as well with people who exhibit no apparent emotion. The situation is more cut-and-dried for him, more logical and systematic.

BMW's Gold Mine Assessment

Needs assessments are carried out at different levels of the sales process. Sometimes it is a one-to-one exchange between the salesperson and the customer. Sometimes it is achieved more broadly through market research and in advertising. The market research performed by world-famous automobile maker BMW is a terrific example of assuming difference, investigating in a positive way, implementing findings, and getting results.

In the early 1990s, BMW's buyer profile information had begun to show a slight increase in women buyers—not the traditional target market for high-performance luxury cars. BMW decided to learn more about women—as consumers, as car buyers, as people, as parents, as workers.

Between 1992 and 1994, BMW of North America gathered information from a variety of sources and in a variety of ways. Every aspect of BMW was investigated from the female perspective: the retail environment, the actual car, communication, dealerships, advertising, service and repair, sales and service training, customer service. Their conclusion? A potentially huge marketing opportunity existed. The ultimate outcome? A 7 percent increase in female purchasers in three years (a much greater increase than other automobile makers experienced.)

The key finding that the marketing people discovered as they talked to women-only focus groups was that both genders used the same words to talk about different concepts. Safety to women meant kid-safe, durable, tough construction, air bags, and antilock brakes. To men, safety tended to have more to do with driving at high speeds on curving roads.

A second vital piece of information that BMW discovered was that men are not as open verbally as women are, particularly about their dissatisfaction. They tend to just bite the bullet. Given the opportunity to be taken seriously and treated respectfully, the women in the focus groups were very articulate about their needs, wishes, thoughts, feelings, likes, and dislikes. And what BMW ultimately found was that making the changes that women suggested increased the satisfaction of both genders.

This carefully planned and expertly implemented needs assessment resulted in enormous changes across the board, from the placement of radio controls to the printed promotional materials. BMW asked, listened, and took action—and got results.

Women Assessing Men's Needs

With male customers, women in sales generally won't have to stretch to understand their stated and unstated needs. Men's wants are usually clearly stated. Their motivations are often less complex than women's. The sales professional's challenge will be to focus more on men's overt wants in terms of the product and the sales process.

Research shows that women are not as skilled in communicating product knowledge, particularly in the mechanical or technical product and service area. If they don't have the depth of knowledge or the command of the industry lingo, they can't ask men the questions required for a comprehensive needs assessment.

Reprogramming

As a saleswoman, even before you make a plan to acquire more product knowledge, you may need to adjust your attitude. It is critical to recognize that your male customers may want more and different kinds of information than you or other women would like.

The fact that men and women are interested in different details is a given. But understanding and translating that difference into a sales approach without feeling defensive can be difficult. You must remind yourself that the perception of you as less knowledgeable about products and services than men in sales is just that—a perception. Changing that perception isn't difficult as long as you acknowledge and work at changing your behavior.

The second step in reprogramming is to eliminate any self-doubt you might have about your ability to understand some complex concepts. Women in real estate training often comment, "I just can't do the math part." For years women's lack of ability in math was accepted as fact. We now know that socialization and expectations were responsible for that belief rather than brains or genes. You don't have to set unrealistic goals: "I'll turn into a math whiz if I work at it." Attempt to think neutrally and thereby eliminate the negative thought: "I can raise my math skills a couple of notches by working on them for one hour a week with a math buddy" or "I know I'm smart enough to figure out the different disability policies if I work on it consistently."

Then, of course, you have to do it. You have to acquire that depth of product knowledge. When you have it and use it and are successful, an almost automatic reprogramming takes place. You begin to see yourself as extremely competent. It shows and reinforces your efforts.

Learn about yourself as a learner. Most product training isn't good. Roger Liston, former worldwide director of sales training for Seagate Technology, Inc., says in *Training* magazine, "Most product training buries sales reps in specs and data sheets. But it doesn't teach them what they need to know about the product, much less how to sell it." And most companies recognize that their product training tends to be boring and lecture-based, requiring rote memory that tends to induce sleep. Any type of good training is interactive, uses accelerated learning techniques, and involves participant practice. If you have difficulty using the product information presented, insist on more effective training.

In the meantime, women can get better at figuring out how to individualize the training to and for themselves. Will it work best for you to tape-record the lecture and then replay and outline it? Or should you take notes as you listen and then discuss the information with a colleague? Do you learn better by attempting to present new information to a sales buddy and then get honest feedback about your credibility? Or will role-playing a needs assessment with a couple of tough questions work for you? There are lots of options. Generally speaking, women learn well from interacting with other people, so think about whether the mentor approach applies to you. Being accountable for your own learning is crucial for women in sales.

Know Your Product, Particularly the Male Ones, Inside and Out

Many women in sales believe that they have to prove themselves. They have to know more, be more, and succeed more than men in order to be judged equally. While that belief may be legitimate, female sales professionals need to accept it and *do it* rather than rail against the injustice of it all. Even if you have an impressive depth of knowledge, consider the possibility that you may not be communicating it in the language of men. After all, they will probably be interested in aspects of the product that are different from the ones you are interested in.

In addition to their interest in facts, numbers, and hard data, men as customers may also want to test women as salespeople. Do you really know what you're talking about when you're discussing the effects of virtual memory on total memory needs, or are you just repeating words and concepts that you've learned? Although the male customer may still buy from you if you're cute enough and he knows enough to answer his own questions, that's not the way most women want to succeed in sales.

Become a techie if necessary. Being familiar with Internet resources is a great advantage in sales. You can use the World Wide Web to find out more about your own products and services, about competitors, and about customer's perceptions. You can find experts out there who'll know more about your company's products than the company knows. You'll also be able to do some buzzword and site name-dropping with male customers. They'll be impressed.

Men still outnumber women on the Internet two to one, but women's use is increasing. Aliza Sherman, known on the Web as Cybergrrl, has a mission: to empower women through technology. Her Cybergrrl Web site offers information on software and links to other female-oriented sites. This might be a good place to start.

Be Direct and Specific

When you really don't know the answer to a question, there is nothing wrong with occasionally saying, "I don't know, and I'll find out." Having written material available that you can share with your male customer is useful in this situation. "I don't know the answer to that. Why don't you look in this manual and I'll look in the smaller handbook, and we'll see if we can find it." This is a definite win-win approach that can appeal to the male customer working with a female salesperson.

While a firm, confident acknowledgment that you don't have all the answers is okay, a wavering disclaimer-filled response such as the following is not: "Gosh, I'm sorry, but I'm not quite sure about that. I guess I could ask the manager, but I think he's at lunch. Well, I do know that a lot of people really think leasing is a better way to go. But then there are other people who think you should always buy instead of lease. It has something to do with taxes, I think. No one has ever really asked me before. Personally I lease, but . . ."

Georgia, a reseller of long-distance telephone services, was making an initial face-to-face sales call after several telephone conversations with a male customer, Rafael. His office was impressive, and he was somewhat intimidating in person. Georgia was nervous. The conversation felt more like an interrogation than a needs assessment to Georgia, with the potential customer in charge. She answered most questions quickly and concisely, but feeling more pressured and challenged, she became less confident. She interrupted the barrage, handed Rafael some written material, and said, "Here's some additional information about the cost and the service. I'll call you at the end of the week, after you've had a chance to look it over thoroughly. Then I'll answer any other questions you might have."

Georgia anticipated a dead deal. She thought Rafael had been testing her, and she had failed. But, as she said she would, she called at the end of the week—and got the business. In retrospect, Georgia concluded that her approach in concluding the needs assessment with Rafael, although not perfect, worked much better than the outcome she avoided: deteriorating into stumbling, rambling, imprecise attempts to convey the requested information.

For female sales professionals, just about anything is better than being overly apologetic, passive, vague, and rambling during the needs assessment. (Only faking it is worse.) If you don't know, you did know but forgot, or you don't even want to know, find out now. Find a way to keep notes so that the information will be handy in the future. But whatever you do, *don't* apologize for not knowing.

April, a lawyer, has a great way of preserving credibility with male clients when she doesn't have the answer. She found that men are less likely to accept "I don't know" or "I'll find out" than women. The first time a male client asked her for information she didn't have, she escorted him down the hall to the firm's impressive law library and said, "We can find all the answers to all the questions right here. I have assistants to handle it." From then on, when a question was asked that she couldn't answer, all she had to do was point knowingly in the direction of the library.

How Can Men Readily Assess the Needs of Women?

Demonstrating that you view women as intelligent consumers is the key to assessing their needs. David Ogilvy, founder of one of the world's largest advertising agencies, many years ago said, "The consumer is not a moron. She is your wife." Even in the current era of social change, some men still think they are superior to women in many areas, including intelligence. This mind-set is untenable according to management gurus like Tom Peters, author of *In Search of Excellence* and *The Circle of Innovation*. Women currently account for $3 trillion worth of purchasing decisions a year, and Peters predicts that women will be the future primary purchasers of almost every good and service.

If you still subscribe to that old mind-set, an attitude adjustment is in order. After quoting a myriad of statistics, a recent promotional letter for a Marketing to Women Congress pointed out, "Women as a buying force are more than a trend. They are your business's future. It's imperative that your company be able to communicate and interact effectively with women." And for men in sales, your company is you.

Listening Without Filtering

One of the obstacles that many men face when listening to women is the presence of a psychological filter that automatically seems to dismiss any information in opposition to the man's viewpoint. A salesman overheard the following conversation between a couple shopping in a jewelry store. She said, "I really think I'd like diamond studs, maybe a half carat, for my birthday." He said, "You're not a diamond kind of person. You're more the outdoorsy type." For whatever reason—cost, taste, opinion—the male customer dismissed his wife's request as if he hadn't even heard it.

This kind of situation can be tricky for the salesman. He looked at the woman carefully and noticed that she wasn't wearing any diamond jewelry although she did have a pearl ring and a wedding band. But she was definitely looking at the diamonds. What should he do? Is it best to approach the couple and ask the woman if she'd like to see some of the diamond earrings? Does he assume the man is paying and so wait until they move toward the man's preference? Does he take the initiative to move the woman away from the diamonds and toward some pearl earrings? Or does he do the same thing her male companion did—ask her what she'd like to see and then tell her something else would be better?

This male sales professional needs to take this female customer seriously. He should ask her what she is interested in, listen to what she says, hear what she says, and act as if he hears what she says. He should show her what she wants to see without making assumptions about her or the couple or who is paying. She wants diamond earrings. The salesperson has diamond earrings—all sizes. There is at least an initial fit, so he should go for it. This kind of situation will be discussed more fully in chapter 10.

Ask More, Tell Less

For men, asking the right questions is the key to the needs assessment. The questions need to be focused, personalized to the customer, and related to the current circumstance. "Just out of curiosity . . ." is never a good beginning to a question—at least not for female customers. Your curiosity is unimportant. What is important—to her and, theoretically, to you—are her needs.

At a different level of needs assessment, Ruth's Chris Steak House, a national restaurant chain that began as an entrepreneurial venture, used gender as one of the variables in their recent customer needs/satisfaction survey. They found that men and women viewed the restaurant's food, ambience, and service similarly. However, just the fact that the male-oriented establishment cared about women's opinions and also featured its female founder in subsequent ads will surely increase female clientele.

Women want to be understood. Men may want to be understood as well, but they will be less likely to feel discounted as a customer if you don't convey understanding. The best way you can convey your interest to women is to ask relevant questions: "What is the audience you would like to target with this program?" "How experienced are they with an interactive computer format?" "What would you like to accomplish by buying new office furniture?"

Random probing—as Jay Chalmers calls unplanned, unfocused, impersonal surveys—is a potential disaster. The female client will feel vulnerable and defensive if she doesn't think that the questions are focused on her specific needs. The outcome? The client disappears.

To eliminate the impression of competitiveness and the consequence of customer defensiveness, avoid the *why* question. It has negative implications. For example, "Why do you prefer the Intel stock over Motorola?" may come across as disapproving even if not intended as such. Using *how, what, where,* and *when* instead will avoid the problem. "How did you decide on Intel stock over

Motorola?" or "What do you particularly like about Intel?" are only slightly different questions, but they come across as more interested and less disapproving.

Following up the questions you ask with a paraphrase or reflection of feeling solidifies the perception that you care about the customer, that you are truly listening and hearing what she says, that you are taking her seriously, and that you are sincere about trying to find the fit that is best for her. You might ask, "What do you need from a bank that you're not getting now?" The customer may respond, "I want easier access to credit, I want a personal relationship with a high-level executive as well as with the loan officer, and I want clear, continuing information about what the best options are for my business." You could combine the reflection of feeling with a paraphrase, and your client would feel magnificently understood: "Sounds as if you're determined to find a bank that can provide strong relationships, available credit, and good customer education." Notice that you are not rushing in to tell her that your fabulous ABC Bank can give her exactly what she wants. No, you're going slow. You're working to make her feel understood.

Fine-Tuning the Assessment

Both men and women need to make some improvements in their approach to needs assessment of the opposite sex.

Women can

- accept that many men think women don't have the right quality and quantity of product knowledge. They can work at altering their perception rather than defending themselves;
- become learners, so they can acquire the information needed to be seen as credible;
- communicate more quantitatively, more specifically, more directly, and briefly when talking about products and services;

• use more male lingo, whether it's about sports, business, a product, or the Internet;
• eliminate an overly apologetic, rambling approach. Instead, they can cut to the chase.

Men can

• listen with full attention and retention, working at retaining the information even if they don't agree or think the customer's comment is accurate. They should not filter out the essential content;
• ask questions that will help them understand the customer and make her feel understood;
• ask about the customer's wants, needs, opinions, and beliefs;
• decrease the ratio of telling to asking;
• eliminate the *why* question.

Chapter 8
The Presentation Dance—
Everybody Does It Differently

The presentation. The words bring forth mental pictures of all kinds: a waiter ceremoniously lifting the domed glass lid covering the beautifully browned and garnished pheasant; a debutante, on the arm of her father, curtsying deeply to a large audience of friends and family; a new-concept motorcycle being rolled out to the amassed trade media. Then there is you, standing up perhaps, spectacularly groomed and impeccably dressed, looking out confidently at your audience of twenty people with an overhead projector buzzing softly next to you, and charts and graphs neatly stacked to hand out. Or perhaps you do your presentations sitting down at a conference table with one or two people. You wear khakis and a button-down shirt. You never use charts. You always present as a team. You only present one-on-one? Or perhaps you think a presentation means any and all modes of explaining your services or product to potential clients, formal or informal, brief or lengthy.

When we interviewed different professionals who sold a variety of products and services, we found that they viewed and conducted the presentation in many different ways. What our salespeople had in common, however, was their belief that the presentation was not the make-it-or-break-it event of the selling process. They tended to think that by the time they arrived at the presentation phase, the sale was a sure thing—unless they really goofed it up or the organization totally changed gears or the competition suddenly dropped their price or the decision-maker dropped dead.

The salespeople we talked with thought that if they hadn't made a good first impression, they wouldn't have gotten any further than the front door. They also thought if they hadn't conveyed that they really understood the needs of the business during the needs assessment, they wouldn't have reached the presentation stage.

The example used in chapter 1 concerning the stockbroker who cold-called me (Judy) demonstrates an approach that never even attempted to establish rapport or build a relationship. He started out by saying, "I'm Michael Smith, a stockbroker for Merrill Lynch. You don't know me. I got your name from a list of former clients of Merrill Lynch." What a relief. This salesman whom I didn't know was not going to pretend to be my friend or, even worse, ask the dreaded question: "How are you today?"

Michael then went directly to the assumed need. "Today, with the stock market dropping so precipitously, would you be interested in making a conservative investment with your money?" When I responded positively, he went on to give a brief presentation on the investment he was selling. It worked. No relationship, a correctly assumed need, followed by a presentation, a close, and excellent follow-up. The presentation alone doesn't make the deal.

The sales professionals we interviewed all agreed that when making a presentation, the ability to adapt to the audience is the single most important factor. The audience may be male or female, young or old, experienced or inexperienced, professionals or laypersons, but adapting to each subgroup of customers is essential. When a group is all one age or gender or occupation, the task is less onerous. But in this era of multiculturalism, gender equity, and cross-functional teams, a homogeneous audience is unlikely.

Sales professionals now present to larger and more heterogeneous groups than in the past. The architect sells the school design to male and female teachers and administrators, parents and school board members, students and community leaders. Salespeople in insurance sell to men and women, young and old, Hispanic and Anglo, entrepreneurs and English teachers, rich and poor. However, specifically different approaches to the presentation may be required depending on your gender and that of your audience.

Gendersell Generalities

We recently witnessed a presentation at its worst. Sylvia was presenting to an all-male group. She was selling bottled water service to the largest division of a medium-sized national organization. The corporate office was in the same location as the division. If she sold the division, she had a good chance of selling the whole organization. She knew the general manager from years ago when he was coming up the ranks and she was just starting out. That is what got her in the door. She knew no one else among the fifteen or so men present and didn't introduce herself or shake hands with any of them prior to the presentation.

She began: "I know you wouldn't want me to bother each of you individually, which is why I asked Sam to let me talk to all of you together." The lights went off. The visuals came up. The history of her company, the different prices and sizes of water bottles were all in tiny type on transparencies. Some serious snoozing took place.

Someone asked if she sold coffee service in addition to the bottled water. Sylvia responded affirmatively but kept on with the presentation. Another man, in response to the coffee question, commented, "It would save John a lot of time and effort to have the same company do all the water and coffee service." She made no comment but went on with the presentation. She concluded: "Does anyone have any questions?" No one did. She left without asking for the business, without a call to action, without planning a next meeting with Sam. After she left, no comments were made about Sylvia, her product or service, or her presentation. To all intents and purposes, she had disappeared.

We have seen a man do the same thing with a primarily female audience. He was presenting an overview of "The Manager as Coach" in an attempt to sell a full training program to representatives of various corporations. His stories focused on team sports. His examples illustrated male management successes. His quotes were drawn from male military or sports leaders. The audience became restless and clearly was not attentive to his pitch. He never knew what happened, but he didn't succeed in selling his idea, his product, or his services to this audience of women. Why? Because his presentation was targeted to men.

Though men can do a bad job of presenting to a male audience and women can do a bad job of presenting to a female audience, the chances of poor performance increase when the gender line is crossed. In general, when giving a presentation, women are viewed as less credible and knowledgeable than men, usually by men but to some extent by women. What women say is remembered less well. Sadly, these scenarios occur even when men and women are introduced with similar credentials and have the same level of speaking ability.

It becomes clear that women have to work harder to close the gap. Survey comments validate this fact: "Maybe it's a stereotype, but they [women] don't seem knowledgeable." "They appear incompetent." "They can't just state the facts." Other perceptions particularly applicable to the presentation stage are that women in sales lack the confidence to "really step up to the plate." They are viewed as soft-spoken and too indirect, or they are viewed as trying too hard, being overly intense, and talking too much.

On the other hand, men are consistently viewed as credible: "They have the facts. They get to the point." "They do a good job acting knowledgeable even if they're not." "They're more informed on technical, thinking aspects of a product." Perceptions that are particularly relevant to the presentation stage are that men may lack the style and ability to engage an audience. They can become talking heads quickly, without involving the presentation participants. Survey respondents also commented on salesmen's tendency to talk down to an audience or sometimes to act arrogant or superior.

Our research, as well as studies by J. D. Power, an international marketing information company, point out that saleswomen are viewed as more honest than salesmen. "When they make the pitch, they tell you the truth" is a typical comment from survey respondents. Other common ones include "Women are more trustworthy" and "They're generally more ethical." In contrast, men are often viewed as self-serving and expedient, saying whatever they need to say to get the customer to buy, whether it's factual or not. Some representative comments include "Men will trick or mislead you"; "I have an inclination to distrust male salespeople"; "Honesty is secondary to the sale."

During presentations, women need to focus on increasing perceived credibility, while men need to concentrate on increasing perceived integrity. Although there are other aspects of the presentation that can be improved by both men and women, success will be most dramatically increased by altering women's perceived expertise and men's perceived honesty.

How Can Women Increase Their Credibility as Presenters?

When interviewed about their presentations, male and female sales professionals seemed to validate the research. Two of the women, both in their twenties and in male dominated fields, recognized the need to come across as authoritative.

Lara Serbin, an architect, often gives solo presentations to large groups of diverse people. She is selling her design as well as her ongoing consulting services during construction. She says she makes a point of keeping the focus off her and on facts, information, and numbers. She wears her hair somewhat severely and very simple, tailored clothes with little adornment. She says she talks the construction business lingo in order to do what she calls "macho presenting." She finds that this approach works best to build credibility with both men and women.

Lara finds that coming across as personable, conveying her own genuine enthusiasm for the project, and demonstrating to the audience that she has listened and understands their uniqueness tends to draw in the women who might not connect with her "macho" style. She notices that she can easily come across as genuine, but she does have to work at coming across as knowledgeable.

Sarah Calfee Shannon sells industrial fasteners and systems for Copper State Bolt and Nut. That means she sells nuts, bolts, and other means of keeping things together, such as electronic equipment, exercise equipment, and seatbelts. She said her number one goal in the presentation is to come across as educated and knowledgeable.

Sarah has chosen to make end users, product engineers, her point of entry rather than the Purchasing Department. These engineers are usually men who really do know it all, so she gets on the manufacturing floor with them and proceeds to look, talk, and ask a lot of questions. By the time she makes a presentation, either to them or to the Purchasing Department, she knows what she is talking about because the product engineers have told her exactly what they need to solve their problems.

Rather than building credibility with a slick businesswoman look, Sarah achieves it by wearing business casual so that she fits in with the people she is calling on. She wears khakis and button-downs with low-heeled shoes. She looks like one of them. Remember that perceived similarity increases liking, comfort, and influence. It works for her.

Both women are using some good techniques to come across as knowledgeable in their presentations. Their ideas as well as some additional techniques, help to increase the impact of the sales presentation for women sales professionals with primarily male audiences.

Build Credibility—Borrow the Look and Sound of Power

Many women sales professionals who have been selling for a long time may feel somewhat resentful when the suggestion is made to borrow power. When you are more knowledgeable than most men in the field, why should you have to prove it over and over again? Unfortunately, old stereotypes die hard. Credibility is usually a comparative measure. How much experience does she have? What is her background in construction? Is she really smart, or is she a wannabe who'll flake out? Is she smiling so much and being so friendly to discourage men from asking the tough questions? Does she really know what she's talking about? Does she know more than I know? That's not good, either.

The young women we talked to, Lara and Sarah, take it as a given that they have to prove themselves. They're young, they're female, and they work in fields still nontraditional for women. Perhaps in ten years they won't see things quite the same way. But for now, working at credibility is okay, and the following tips will probably prove useful to many saleswomen.

Both Lara and Sarah dress more like the men they work with and the men in their audience than like women. They still wear makeup and jewelry. They just take the focus off their femaleness in order to decrease the impact of the sometimes negative female stereotype. This is a great way to borrow power.

During a sales presentation to a known resistant, arrogant group of high-level male attorneys, I (Judy) decided to open on the offense instead of coming up with a needed defense later. I introduced myself and briefly stated the credentials that would most likely impress this group: a Ph.D., universities attended, books published, and major corporate clients. I started the presentation with these words: "Gentlemen, I know that you are a learned, intelligent, and powerful group of attorneys who are experts in the law and perhaps many other areas as well. Right now I would like you to consider the possibility that I may know more about today's topic—conflict between the genders in the workplace—than you do. I certainly don't know more about the practice of law or managing a large law firm, but I am an expert on gender and the workplace. I'd like you to listen and keep your minds open to the possibility that what I have to tell you is accurate, current, and right."

I saw some smiles and even some slightly sheepish grins. I had gained their attention and, at least for the moment, had gently detached them from their instant superiority without sounding hostile, defensive, or arrogant myself. In other words, I had built credibility. They asked questions and treated me as an expert. And they listened.

Borrowing power from known male experts is another way to increase perceived expertise. When we are selling ideas to a group, we often use this tactic. One way is to support our opinions with quotes from top experts and reliable sources. For example, you might say, "George Simons, coauthor of *Transcultural Leadership* and an intercultural communications expert, believes that gender difference is the biggest cultural gap that exists, the root paradigm of difference." Or you might comment that excellence guru Tom Peters believes women have spent years learning how to play men's games, but now it's time for men to learn how to play the women's game.

Use Some Humor

Particularly when presenting to a predominantly male group, using humor early on is a great icebreaker. Men often say that women take themselves too seriously, try too hard, and work too much to prove themselves. If you can introduce some humor early on, you'll quickly alter these preconceived ideas held by your audience. People who can lighten up, particularly during stressful situations such as a presentation, are seen as confident and competent even if they're not. The belief is that you must know what you're doing if you can joke when times are tough.

One method that works well is to tap into a real situation that happened inside your client's business, then tie it into your presentation; for example, "I want you to know that I brought along three technical advisers this morning to be sure all this upscale, high-tech presentation equipment does its job. I understand that Joe Smith from your company, who's sitting right here today, had a total technical meltdown last week presenting to the top guns at Motorola." The Joe Smith story has undoubtedly made the rounds and is, in the men's competitive arena, a surefire punchline. I (Judy) often check ahead with the man I'm going to single out to be sure he's okay with it and is prepared for it. I would never use the same kind of put-down humor with women.

Unless you have already built strong credibility in sales or are already seen as overly competent, inaccessible, or pushy, don't use self-deprecating humor when presenting to men. When you jokingly say, "You all know me by now, but I want to let you know that you don't have to worry about problems today. I brought along three technical advisers this morning—one to help me find my way here, one to hook up all this presentation equipment, and one to rescue me if it all falls apart," you reinforce beliefs that you don't know what you're doing. On the other hand, female audiences might find that self-deprecating humor funny. They recognize it because it's their style of humor, and they sense a similarity with you and subsequently connect.

Another good way to use humor in a presentation is to occasionally throw a cartoon up on your overhead or insert one in your handouts. Bring along hard copies because audience members often ask for one, particularly if the cartoon fits them and their business. Put your name, company name, and phone number on the cartoon, and you have some instant promotional material.

Use Male Lingo and Topics

When presenting to a predominantly male group use jargon, male words, and business lingo. Lara, the architect mentioned earlier, finds that she impresses men and women alike by using construction trade words rather than a layperson's vocabulary. She talks about "daylighting the hole" instead of "drilling the hole," about furring strips instead of wood strips.

Know what is current in the sports realm and make some reference to it. Use a sports story about a local hero or a company hero. Read the local paper and tie current business news into your presentation. Your male audience will conclude that you are "with it."

Be Direct and Specific

Women's tendency to be overly apologetic can show up vividly in a presentation: "I'm sorry that we didn't get started on time, but you know how that goes sometimes on a Monday morning. And I'm, well, not exactly a—you know—morning person." If you are late, use some humor to get started and forget the apology: "The morning people out there are probably getting a little restless waiting for me to get going, but you night people are probably glad to have had three more minutes of wake-up time."

Particularly in the presentation stage of the sales process, being concise, precise, and to the point is critical. Vagueness, rambling, and too many details give the impression that you don't know what you're talking about even if you're a whiz kid. Up to this point in the sales process, you can get away with some imprecision, including indirect, casual speech that contains a few "umm-mms," "you knows," and "whatevers." Now you can't.

Write a script and memorize it, using notes or an outline of the main points. Rehearse in front of a mirror or practice in front of an audience of friends, family, or male coworkers. Join Toastmasters, an organization that teaches public speaking. Be open to constructive feedback. Tell your practice audience how you can receive feedback best, so you can increase the likelihood that you will hear what they say and use it. A presentation always needs to be exact and exacting.

Decrease Emotional Intensity

Because women often feel and express emotions more intensely than men, dropping the level of verbal and nonverbal vividness will often be better received by men. Since you'll still be matching women by at least being somewhat emotional, they won't be alienated by the drop in intensity.

Recent research demonstrates that men have a lower tolerance than women to the physiological changes that occur with intense emotion. Consequently, what they perceive as an excess of expressed emotion can make men feel uncomfortable in personal and professional relationships.

If you're emotionally expressive, men as coworkers or as an audience may see you as a lot of work. The implied expectation for them is that they respond with the same level of emotional intensity as you do. Since they are reluctant to do this, the common reaction is to back off and become even less involved.

To avoid this problem, use adjectives that are slightly less superlative—"wonderful" instead of "fantastic," "excellent" instead of "awesome," "great" instead of "fabulous." Use feeling words that are also less intense in emotion: "enthusiastic" instead of "thrilled," "slightly stressed" instead of "freaked out." The same principles apply with nonverbal behavior. Frequent pleasant smiles are better than constant wide grins; moderate facial and hand gestures and occasional stillness are better than exaggerated movements. Finally, stand up when making any presentation. We have never seen men present sitting down, but women do it frequently. Women in particular need to look in charge, in control. Sitting doesn't cut it.

What Can Men Do Differently When Presenting to Women?

Steven Dodenhoff, who sells services for MicroAge, says that he thinks conveying sincerity and trustworthiness is the most important aspect of the presentation. Although he acknowledges that the first impression is the most crucial stage of the selling process, he thinks that the presentation stage is where everything is pulled together. This is where it should be revealed that you are an honest person who pulls no punches and that you understand what the client says they need. This is a critical aspect of men selling to women.

Wyatt Earp is a sales professional with New York Life. He was so excited to sell benefits right from the start that when we were interviewing him about presentations, he was giving one. He views the presentation stage as the solution stage. This is where he tells people the solution to what he views as their disturbance.

Wyatt says what he does least well is schmooze. Sometimes he is so sure of the fit and so eager to have the client see what he sees clearly that he cuts to the chase and delivers the presentation too soon—particularly when he's working with women. In all likelihood Wyatt comes across as too slick, too smooth, and too pushy with women even though he may be completely honest.

Let's look at some techniques that men can use to increase female customers' perception that they are sincere sales professionals.

Build the Trust

Because many women are not used to being taken seriously as customers, they are often more suspicious to start off with than the average salesman deserves. Nonetheless, those frequently prede-termined attitudes mean that the male presenter needs to do a better-than-average job of appearing personally interested in the client and genuine in telling her why he thinks this is the best product for her. A presenter who is too slick and smooth can appear too impersonal.

Wyatt, the insurance salesman, mentioned that he was basically a shy kind of guy. He doesn't come across that way and has clearly worked hard to overcome his fears. Paradoxically, if he let his shyness become slightly more visible, he might increase women's perception of him as sincere.

In a presentation, occasional stumbling or bumbling, a bit of self-deprecating humor, and less industry or general motivational jargon will work wonders. To avoid the canned sound, avoid the pat phrases, the rah-rah stuff, the predictable, trite approaches that sound so phony: "Joan, this will be the best decision of your life, and I know you'll never regret it." "What can I do to get you to buy this car today?" "No, I'm not selling cosmetic surgery. I'm selling an opportunity for youth and beauty." "We're selling success." Many women think comments like this are pure bull. (Men may think they're bull as well but will usually accept them as part of the game.)

In the past, female customers have had less opportunity to work with saleswomen, whom they tend to trust more than their male counterparts. But as more women become salespeople in a broader variety of industries, men will have to come across as more honest and less manipulative to win women's business.

Avoid Giving Advice Unless Asked

To avoid giving advice may seem contradictory, particularly because the presentation stage is often viewed as the right time to give the customer your recommendations. However, there is always the possibility of appearing different in the presentation than you did when meeting one-on-one. Perhaps you'll seem more distant or paternal or oddly authoritarian. By making suggestions that are always framed as *responses* to your female client's request, you can avoid that impression. For example, "You asked my opinion about whether it was wise to continue your disability policies now that you're almost sixty-two and in perfect health, so I investigated and here's what I found." By saying, "From what you've told me, it seems that the smaller model would fit your needs best. Here's how I came to that recommendation," the salesperson includes the client as a partner in the advice.

Telling the female client or the audience what they should, ought, or must do doesn't work unless it is in response to a specific query: "What do you think we should buy?" Only then should you jump in and say exactly what you think—but still tie it into your knowledge about the customer.

Talk About People and the Product or Service

Because women are more interested than men in feelings and relationships, show *people* and not just parts of products in your visuals. Recognizing that women are the big purchasers of houses, the Martz Advertising agency recently produced a campaign showing very few actual houses or lots, views, or golf courses; instead it showed lots of people of all ages doing varied activities together outside of the barely visible houses in the background.

In your presentation, show pictures of people like the women you are selling to using your products and services. Build in identification. About Women and Marketing Inc., the Boston-based research and publishing company, has found that women prefer to see and hear about "real" women who are similar to themselves. They are turned off by the supermodels, supermoms, and supercareer chargers. Be sure your materials, overheads, and promotional materials show many different women using the product or service—not just a token shot. Highlight regular-looking men and women in the workplace: clerical people, management people, factory workers, technicians—gray-haired, a bit overweight, in suits or in casual business clothes.

When presenting, be sure you use the female pronoun once in a while unless the product is used exclusively by men. Women are unlikely purchasers of jockstraps for themselves or for a gift, but they may be discerning buyers of almost anything else that men use or buy. The unwieldy "he or she" doesn't have to be used, but be sure to alternate the sex of your pronouns.

In their genuine zeal to come across as egalitarian, many men end up inadvertently patronizing women in a presentation. A government official, selling legislation to a largely male audience, demonstrated this well. In an attempt to appeal to the few women in the audience, the presenter referred several times to his female boss as a "sharp lady," and a "very sharp gal." Although his intentions were good, the impact wasn't.

Increase the Use of Feeling Words

The presentation may be the only connection you have with some of the female decision-makers. Speaking their language is important. The language of emotion is not the only language of women, but they do tend to use it more often than men. Using feeling words will therefore resonate. Again, don't overdo it. "You women will just love the feel of this car" may not work as well as "Women in particular have commented that they really enjoy the feel of the car when they drive it. Its solidness says stability and security."

It is important to accept the "gut" as an important aspect of all buying decisions. Men as customers simply don't acknowledge the emotional aspect as much as women, but they certainly have a "gut" reaction. Women will appreciate the salesman's use of feeling words, and men won't be turned off even though they themselves may not speak that language. Men and women will both be turned off by an exaggerated approach. For example, don't say, "You're going to experience a real rush when you sign the papers on this land. You're going to feel on top of the world."

Notice how the women you work with use feeling words in everyday work-related conversation. Then attempt to imitate that ratio in the presentation. If you're not comfortable with that level of frequency, then lessen it.

Perfect Presentations

Perfection in presenting probably doesn't exist, so constantly improving presentation skills is critical for both men and women in sales. Although many people think the sale is a done deal before the presentation even begins, it in fact can easily change the direction of the deal, particularly to a new or different audience.

Women can improve their presentation skills by

- borrowing power to present. Look and sound similar to your male audience and/or quote prominent men in the industry to support your position. Or bring one along to co-present, with you playing the major role;
- lightening up and learning to be comfortable using spontaneous or relevant nonsexual humor with a male audience;
- doing whatever it takes to be precise and specific, such as charts, graphs, and notes written on the transparency frames.

You want a tight, concise presentation before you open for questions or comments;
• keeping emotions moderate in words, gestures, and facial expressions.

Men can improve their presentation skills by

• coming across as genuine, caring, and sincere. Treat the female customer with clear respect, recognizing that she may be less trusting than your average male customer;
• avoiding an overly slick, too confident, or cocky presentation style. A little genuine anxiety can look appealing as well as sincere;
• presenting as a business partner, not as an authoritarian controller. Avoid such words as should, must, have to, never, always, and absolutely. Remember, you are recommending, not commanding;
• including pictures or words about people using the products or services you are presenting rather than focusing on the features of the product;
• getting emotional. Use feeling words, talk about emotional events, and relate to women's internal self as well as their external self;
• involving your female audience in the presentation.

Chapter 9
Hard Sell or Soft Close?

In its simplest form, closing the sale means getting written or verbal agreement to trade a product or service for either money or another product or service. Closing the deal may also mean mutually agreeing on an idea and coming up with ways to implement it.

However, since "closing" has such a negative connotation, we prefer to use the phrase "opening the sale" to describe this process. "Opening" conveys endless opportunities while "closing" represents limited chances. And because the opening of service rather than the closing of choices will be implied when the salesperson asks for the business, the customer will feel less pressured at this time.

A great example of opening the sale was described by Harry, a running buddy. He and his eighty-three-year-old mother, Freda, were shopping for a new car for her. After a few negative experiences at dealerships, they found a saleswoman who was a great fit for Freda. The entire transaction went smoothly and quickly, with Freda and the sales professional doing most of the talking to each other.

Harry was generally pleased, but what really impressed him was the fact that the saleswoman spent an hour and a half with his mother *after the contract was signed,* taking her for a drive and showing her how all the buttons and switches worked. She went so far as to open the hood, show Freda the engine, explain to her how to use jumper cables if necessary. All this attention took place following the sale, to a customer who undoubtedly will not be buying more cars in her lifetime. Therefore, the follow-through must have come from caring or from feeling optimistic that Harry would be buying more cars in his lifetime even if his mother wouldn't be.

Gendersell Generalities

While there are exceptions to every rule, men are generally more confident than women in the closing stage of selling. Men have little problem asking for the business. In fact, they have more of a problem *not* asking for it. For example, when we were presenting a workshop for a local automobile dealer, we advised the salesmen never to say to female customers, "What can I do to get you to buy the car today?" They had been taught by the dealer to ask that question at least three times in their first contact with the customer. Our suggestion was almost unacceptable to the male audience. Even when I warned that those dreaded words might kill the deal with female customers, the men weren't willing to concede. Their traditional training about competition—making it happen now and closing the deal as fast as possible—made them unreceptive to a more flexible closing strategy.

There are many reasons that men are more confident than women when asking for the business. They may have more experience. Although the number of women in sales is growing—their total number in 1982 was less than 7 percent but was 23 percent in 1995—many haven't had the same amount of experience with the resulting confidence to ask for the business.

Men also are less likely than women to feel the same fear of rejection. Perhaps because men have been the traditional initiators of romantic relationships, they have become less sensitive to rejection. For many men, attempting to close the sale is no big risk. It's part of the game.

Women are generally more uncomfortable with risk as well as rejection than men. After all, if you never try to close the sale, you never have to risk anything and won't get rejected. Michael Widdows, manager of sector operations for Glaxo Wellcome, a pharmaceutical company, says that one of the reasons saleswomen are so successful in his industry is that they never have to close the deal. The whole process, he explains, is based on successful relationships with physicians, pharmacists, and managed health care executives. Salespeople build the relationship from the first cold call to an ongoing friendship, hoping that if the customer likes and trusts the sales professional and is convinced of the drug's benefits, he or she will prescribe the particular pharmaceutical product at hand. The salesperson in pharmaceuticals is therefore basically doing education and public relations for a specific medication and is never in the position of asking for the order or being turned down. Doctors who believe in the drug will prescribe it.

Widdows also mentioned that the physical appearance of the salesperson and opposite-sex attraction seems to be a big factor in pharmaceutical sales. He suggests that good-looking men and women have an advantage; the men have an easier time getting through to the main man through his usually female receptionist, while the women do better scheduling time and sales opportunities with male physicians and pharmacists once they have seen her in person. As sexist as these scenarios may sound, they are facts of life.

Not surprisingly, each gender is often critical of how the other closes and follows through. Consequently, men and women in sales generally don't want to learn each other's closing methods. We strongly suggest rethinking this attitude. By adopting some of the other gender's approaches and adapting to the customer, you will definitely increase your closing ratio with the opposite sex.

Closing the Sale for Women: Just Do It

Thinking differently about closing, risk, and rejection is a form of reprogramming. If women in sales can see the close as a service they provide their customers instead of a pushy request, it will become easier. If they can erase the association of risk and rejection with the close, they might be able to clinch the deal more readily.

Another way to think differently about this stage is to see it as the first step in providing customer service. You wouldn't think of signing a sales contract without delivering the product. Similarly, the female salesperson might begin to think that once she makes a sales presentation of any kind, not following through by asking for the business is not completing her responsibility to the client.

Make the Interaction a Win-Win

Most sales outcomes should be a win-win, meaning that the customer and the sales professional have made a deal that benefits them both. Using neutral wording that you're comfortable with can help facilitate this situation. "What is your interest level at this time?" may be easier than "Are you ready to make a decision?" "How much time would you like to think about our discussion?" might work better than "Let's finish up the discussion and get down to brass tacks." Determine the wording or phrases that reflect your style, then ask for the business in a confident but comfortable manner.

Women in sales occasionally come across as too intense or too eager to be right with male colleagues, managers, or customers—whether anything is said or not. For example, you may be thinking, "This guy thinks he's going to beat me with his knowledge of numbers. Well, he's wrong. I'll show him up in a hurry." Competing with the customer of either gender just doesn't work. But women should be particularly careful not to one-up male customers. No one likes losing face, and there are still strong traditional attitudes in the marketplace about gender—and one is that men, in particular, don't like being shown up publicly by women.

Calculate, Then Take Risks

Women often aren't sure enough of their own instincts or knowledge base to say to themselves, "Yes, the time is right, and this is the best approach with this person." This can put the sales professional in the position of not asking for the sale because she is never confident that she has enough information.

The magnitude of risk, perceived or real, can be greatly diminished by gathering information ahead of time. When deciding the right time for the close, the salesperson should take into account the players involved, the company and its needs, the product and its benefits, the sales process, and her own particular strengths. But learning to err on the side of taking more rather than less risk is a good exercise in development of your skills.

A female sales representative for British Air tells a funny story about a particular close early in her sales career. She was attempting to sell her company's services to a male decision-maker in a large British company. She was delivering a lengthy pitch with enthusiasm and gusto when the potential customer interrupted her to say, "Why should I buy from you?" She dropped to her knees in a prayerful position and said, "Because if you do, I'll be able to keep my job." She took a huge risk, albeit uncalculated, and it worked. She made the sale and left a memorable impression.

We're not suggesting that begging for the business is the right way to go, but taking an occasional calculated risk is. Because many men see themselves as women's protectors, suggesting that you need their business can sometimes work. You may not be comfortable with this approach, just as some women may not be comfortable with a flirtatious approach, but each is good to keep on the back burner.

Find the risks that you are willing to take. Try asking for the business early in the rapport-establishing stage. Say, for example, "I'm going to make my understanding of your company's needs my top priority for the next month. I'll be prepared to tell you very specifically how we can increase your customers' satisfaction by the end of this month. I'd like you to be prepared to make a decision by then as well."

How Women Can Fix Up the Follow-Through with Men

Attentiveness to follow-through is a real asset, but many of the women we interviewed had more difficulty figuring out how to maintain relationships with male clients than with female clients. The majority of the women, married or single, felt uncomfortable doing anything social or recreational with their male customers after the sale unless they were team-selling or their customers were team-buying. The only activities they felt comfortable with were visiting the business or plant, sending notes, making phone calls, and sending articles of interest. This can still be a tricky situation for many women, particularly when they're traveling and selling to mostly male clients in unfamiliar settings. Obviously, the fine line between business and pleasure is a rocky terrain that women need to navigate. Our recommendation is to put your efforts toward boosting your *professional* assets with male clients. If your attitude during the follow-up is warm but businesslike, it will be clear that your overtures are purely professional.

Know Potential Product Problems

The saleswoman's job becomes even more difficult after the close because she has to anticipate her male client's needs and wants. Because he'll be more likely to say "no problem" or "all's well," the saleswoman needs to be extra alert to tone and nuance. At the same time she needs to be sure her follow-up doesn't sound nagging or needy: "Are you sure everything is okay?" "You'd let me know if you weren't happy, wouldn't you?" "You aren't just saying that, are you?"

How to do this? Knowing your product and service well can help you determine any concerns, problems, and positive experiences the customer may encounter after the sale. Rather than asking "How's everything going with your new fax machine?" and getting "Fine" as a response, you should ask specific questions based on your experience: "Do you have your fax up and running?" "I know you were interested in batch faxing. Have you used that function yet?" "Many people use the basic fax functions easily and smoothly but don't get around to using some of the more sophisticated ones. I'd like to stop by next week and spend thirty minutes with you or your assistant to be sure you're getting the most out of your fax." In this way you are not asking if the person needs help. You are not suggesting that he is overwhelmed, confused, or underusing the machine. And you are giving him the opportunity to have someone else get the additional training even if he was the purchaser.

Be Direct and Specific

Although both men and women dislike conflict, confrontation, and dissatisfied customers, women seem more uncomfortable when faced with men's anger and frustration than vice versa. When this discomfort leads to a wishy-washy message, many men will see the female salesperson as "flaky." For example, when delivery of a promised computer is delayed, it is better to say, "The computer that we scheduled for delivery on the fifteenth will be here on the twenty-fifth instead. I'm sorry. We will take it directly to your office so you don't have to pick it up," rather than, "Well, it won't be here on the fifteenth, I'm afraid, but we hope it'll be just a few days overdue." It is better to deal directly with the customer's frustration than with the consequences of avoiding it, such as daily status checks and increased dissatisfaction on his part. Assertiveness is the best way to go for follow-up.

Men: Think About Opening the Sale Instead of Closing

If men continue to think of opening the sale instead of closing the sale, as we suggested earlier, they are more likely to go slowly when building the relationship. This approach will work best with most female customers. First, wait for a sign from your female customer, verbal or nonverbal, that she is ready to buy. Next, ask rather than tell. Finally, act in accord. Of course, when you put all those steps together, closing could take a long time. Remember, though, that in selling, people rarely get into trouble by going too slowly, whereas the salesman who goes too fast may not only lose the sale but risks offending the customer. That is trouble.

Ask More, Tell Less

Regardless of what you're selling, asking more and telling or advising less during the close will work particularly well with women. While this is not a hard-and-fast rule, asking conveys that you are not trying to pressure the woman into acceptance, while telling can come across as overpowering: "I can see you love this machine. It's yours. Just sign on the dotted line, and I promise you'll never be sorry."

On the other hand, any number of subtle questions can be used when you're ready to ask for the business: "Where are you in your decision-making process?" "Do you want to talk specifics now about this purchase, or would you rather concentrate on more fact-finding?" "Is there any other information you would like to see before you make a final decision?" If you ask these questions well, your female customer will tell you she is ready to buy.

Act in Accord

At the point of asking for the business, listen carefully to the response and accept it rather than disputing or challenging it. For example, if your closing question is "Would you like more information now about where we go from here to make this purchase happen?" and your female customer responds, "No, I've had it with information today. I'll stop back tomorrow," just say, "Great. I should be here all day, but if you call first, you can be sure I'm in." That's acting in accord. Acting in discord is saying, "There's no time like right now to make a decision" or "You're a smart lady. I'm sure you can handle more information today." Although acting in accord is very simple, it is sometimes a hurdle for men working with women. Perhaps it's the old competitive spirit rearing up at the closing stage of selling.

For Men: Women Want Follow-Through

Women are often more work as customers than men, but if they're happy with your performance, they'll tell the world. They'll extol you and your product or service to men and women alike. But if you fall down on follow-through, you may risk compromising all that you have done up to that point. Also remember that your female customer will probably let everyone know about your poor performance. So whether you think she is a piece of work or a lot of work, be aware that she will also be, in all probability, the primary purchaser of almost everything in the future. You need to do the follow-through to keep her—and everyone she connects with—as a continuing customer.

Keep on Building

For many women, good, long relationships are extremely valuable. They are more inclined than men to turn professional or business relationships into friendships. Building a relationship with a female customer may mean that it will be ongoing; therefore, try to keep in touch if you can. While sending flowers the day after the sale isn't necessary, a call or a note or a personal thank-you is effective and achieves better results than turning the female client over to customer service or, even worse, dropping out of the picture. If you want her to come back to you and your company in the future, stay awake and stay connected.

Closing Comments

For both male and female sales professionals, asking for the business is essential. Yet women have a tendency not to do it at all, and men have a tendency to do it too soon—particularly when they're selling to the opposite sex. Why? The salesperson's own style of closing is at odds with the preferred style of his or her customer.

Both men and women can profit by seeing the close as an integral part of the relationship-building process. Viewing this step as an "opening" will improve both their outlook and their way of asking for the business. Both genders can benefit by taking their time, truly looking for the win-win, and being genuine.

What women can do to improve the close and follow-through with men:

- Just do it. Do whatever it takes to view the closing process as a desirable service that you provide your customer. Then experiment with different methods, at all different stages of the sales process, until you find what works best with men.
- Even if you're resentful that men sometimes perceive women in sales as subpar, resist the urge to let it show directly or indirectly.
- Increase your skills at assessing risk and at taking risks in sales even when there is a low probability of success. Learn how to take rejection impersonally.
- Increase your awareness of how you want to play the "attraction" card—and accept the consequences.
- Plan a solid follow-through even if men don't ask for help or identify problems after the sale.

What men can do to improve their close with women:

- Stay alert to what is going on long after the papers are signed.
- Ask open-ended, purchaser-friendly questions as you move your customer closer to the close.
- S-l-o-w down. Stretch out the whole process from rapport to close, but most important, don't push or press the close. It is better to have her sign next month than never.
- Think about your relationship with the female customer as a potential lifelong connection.

Chapter 10
Selling to Couples:
Navigating the Battlefields

A husband and wife are at the local department store to buy carpeting.

> MARY: Ralph, I want your opinion on the new carpeting. You're going to be living with it, too, and I want to have your honest feedback on what color and texture you would like.
>
> RALPH: Honey, this is your department. I trust your judgment. You just pick what you want.
>
> MARY: I really do want your opinion on this.
>
> RALPH: It really doesn't matter to me, Mary. I want you to be happy.
>
> MARY: (starting to get a little irritable): Ralph, you never give me your input on these kinds of things. You always make me decide. Now I want you to tell me what you think!
>
> RALPH: (sighing, points to a dark orange sample): Well, okay. How about that one? It would match . . .
>
> MARY: (throwing up her hands and saying in complete exasperation): You're kidding, aren't you? I can't believe you would choose that color.

Enter Theresa. Selling to couples is something that Theresa, a top producer with a carpet and tile company, is confronted with every day. On more than one occasion she has had to contemplate whether her job description should read "sales professional" or "marriage counselor."

Indeed, many sectors of the sales field—from real estate and car sales to wedding rings and burial plots—count large numbers of couples as their customers. The potential profits, referrals, and long-term relationships that can result from selling to couples is enormous. But it is also a delicate process that requires sensitivity, perception, and seasoned maneuvering. If a sales professional doesn't understand the potential battle that can erupt when couples are making a major purchase decision together, she may end up alienating or even offending one of the partners. The result is a lost sale.

It is important for a sales professional to take into consideration the many hidden factors at hand when a couple makes a joint purchase. They may have an established relationship and be into power plays. Or they could have just met and are still working out the complex patterns of communication between them. A couple may make buying decisions together (even if one of the partners is not present), or they may make buying decisions separately. Their money may be kept in a joint account, or they may keep separate accounts.

Three-person chemistry always presents a challenge—the "extra wheel" syndrome—and this certainly includes you with any couple you are trying to influence. Once you add a mixture of genders to the sales scenario—plus the hidden baggage each person brings to the table and the pressure everyone feels to make the right purchase decision—you have a potential powder keg.

There are undoubtedly as many differences in the ways couples make buying decisions together as there are individuals who make up these partnerships. Sales professionals must learn to recognize and understand these differences, and how to work with them.

Couples in the War Zone

Couples often feel pressure as they enter the sales arena. It is common for them to anticipate, feel, discuss, or even plan strategies against you, the salesperson. Meanwhile, financial concerns—and money matters are still on top of the heap when it comes to marital spats—inevitably turn up the heat beneath many purchasing decisions. Even when the buildup of such tensions is minimal, it is easy for a couple to anticipate an "us and them" sales scenario.

Adam and Cindy Brooks were married less than one year and made every purchase a joint decision. According to Adam, salespeople tended to focus on him because he was more cautious, asked more serious questions, and looked at the facts. Cindy, on the other hand, was more trusting. If a salesperson was friendly, Cindy was likely to agree to a purchase. Their first major purchase decisions seemed to confirm the perceived threat of the sales office as a war zone.

"Our worst purchasing experience turned out to be our most positive," explains Adam. "It was our first experience with a joint purchase, before we were married. We were buying a car. We spent many difficult months, looking on weekends and evenings, talking to lots of people, and dealing with a lot of salesmen who would mislead us.

"We started out wanting two different things because we had different perceptions of what we were going to buy. I wanted an Infinity G-20, Cindy wanted a Geo Metro. I wanted something sporty, Cindy wanted something less expensive.

"We found that salespeople would present something—anything—that would get us attached to a vehicle. They would show us stuff that was exciting to me, and the price was right for Cindy. We'd be convinced, spend time doing the paperwork, and then they would say the car was going to be about $5,000 more than they had originally said. It was frustrating."

Adam and Cindy eventually ended up avoiding the salesroom by buying their Chrysler LeBaron convertible through a newspaper ad.

"In the final analysis it was less the salesperson and more our process together in looking and decision-making that determined our purchase," concluded Adam. After going through a similar experience with buying a house, this bright young couple seemed to know how to focus on the item to be purchased rather than on the person selling it to them.

"I think that, in either case, if we'd had a salesperson who really listened to what we wanted—*both* of our needs—and had been honest about being able to fit those needs, we would have stayed with that person. Unfortunately, in most cases we found that salespeople tended to "bait" us, getting us excited, and then switched their terms."

This is valuable information for sales professionals. This couple needed to go through an exploration process. They needed to listen to each other, be patient, gather information, and keep on problem-solving until a consensus was reached. The sales professional does, too.

After interviewing numerous couples, we found many different ways that couples make purchasing decisions:

- Bobby takes care of automobiles; Bonnie takes care of furniture. She trusts him; he trusts her.
- Rebecca and Robert make any purchases over $200 together (except clothes). Even if the item is for only one of them (a new car), the person it's for will preshop and then bring in the other only for a final consultation. They keep their finances separate.
- Dan says, "Since money and how it is spent is a major source of contention between many couples, Patty and I have always kept our money separate. We make separate decisions on major purchases, although we do discuss what we are planning to do. We are almost never with a salesperson at the same time, and when we tried buying together as a couple, we found it

difficult to agree. So now we try to avoid it."
• Jeff says, "I make all the major decisions; Sheryl makes all the minor decisions. The major decisions are in the area of philosophy, religion, politics, and art. The minor decisions are cars, houses, and financial products. In fifteen years of marriage, I haven't had to make a single minor decision. Seriously, I trust my wife explicitly. She has bought cars, houses, and landscaping, all without me. She does all the research and interviews, then gives me an overview. For us, it works great."

The fact that every couple is different may seem obvious, and it's nothing new that many couples enter the sales arena with some trepidation about money pressures and preconceived notions about salespeople. Unfortunately, the real challenge for sales professionals is that many couples end up being their own worst enemies when it comes to decision-making—and it's likely to become the sales professional's job to sort things out.

The Sales Professional's Role

The many hidden agendas and unknown hot buttons of a couple's dynamic represent a difficult challenge. Simmering personal tensions over a potential purchase often overheat due to unresolved relationship issues that the couple carries with them. Surprise. This is where your sales professional role takes on an incredibly complex new dimension as couples counselor.

Fortunately, psychologists have been learning about relationship dynamics for decades. I (Judy) have been a therapist for many years. Sound counseling principles can and should be applied by salespeople when dealing with couples. It starts from the moment a couple walks in your door.

One of the things I do up front in counseling is try to establish a common mission. Despite everything else a couple might not agree on, there is always something they have in common that brought them to counseling—or to the marketplace. Whether they want an improved relationship, a washer and dryer, a great vacation getaway, or homeowner's insurance, there is always common ground somewhere.

A good counselor starts by asking both people separately for their point of view: "Let's talk about what's really important to you, Martha." "What's important to you, John?" "Okay, who wants to start?" You are then better able to identify who plays what role in this duo. The "leader" in a particular couple might give you information about who the "decision-maker" is, that is, the one who initiates or the one who dominates in the family. Sometimes one person is a "victim," and the other is the controller.

After a counselor has heard what a couple wants and needs, he or she can pull together the commonalities and summarize them. "So, you both want to argue less and get back to having more meaningful time together." Sounds like counselor talk, right? But, a time-honored key to sales success is always remembering to point out people's similarities. You want them to feel as if they are on the same team. "So then, you both agree that the larger van would take care of both your recreational needs and also the transportation needs for your family."

Conversely, you always get in trouble as a counselor (as well as a salesperson) if you take sides: "John wants to have the potential financial gain of the higher risk stock; Martha, does that seem unreasonable?" By phrasing something in this fashion, Martha's trust is going to take an abrupt nosedive. The same principle holds true in a sales situation.

How do you avoid getting caught in the middle? Try to get a handle on the couple's status as quickly as possible and become aware of where their relationship is at that moment. Marilyn Powers, Ph.D., a practicing therapist for more than twenty years, notes that couples are always in one of three communication stages: a fusion stage, a power struggle stage, or an interdependent stage where the couple is working toward reaching a mutually beneficial solution.

"Be careful about getting caught in the middle where one partner pits the professional against the other," she says. "If faced with this kind of a situation, the sales professional needs to address the issue of unity up front: 'I'm here to be a resource person for both of you. I know the two of you can come up with the best solution for your particular needs.' "

Powers then suggests giving the couple a little space—a time-out—so they can talk alone. When there is a difference of opinion, a couple needs some time to communicate without pressure. If they come to a decision without complete agreement, chances are they'll reverse themselves later. This is good advice for the sales situation as well.

Do you feel competent as a counselor? Probably not. But don't worry—the sales professional doesn't have to have all the answers to a couple's potential problems. But you do need to know that as a salesperson you have the advantage of being an experienced adviser who is outside any power struggle and can reflect back impartially what you hear that is important to the couple.

How to Adapt to Couple Dynamics

Counseling and relationship therapy offer many specific and practical methods to help couples communicate—and make important decisions. Likewise in sales, you must learn to adapt successfully to couple dynamics. This begins by getting the lay of the land—or surveying the potential battlefield—when you first meet a new couple.

It is important to discover quickly, through subtle cues such as eye contact, body language, and tone of voice, whether the couple is in agreement or in conflict. Begin to determine which of the three stages their relationship is in—fused together, in a power struggle, or interdependent. Do they appear to act and feel alike? Are they in competition? Are they comfortable with their differences? Do they work together to find a mutually satisfying solution? Here's how to figure it out:

If a couple is in the fused stage—where they always want to think and feel alike—the sales professional may not be able to get enough details or the correct information. The couple's decision can be made too quickly, and the sale can easily unravel. The fused couple is so quick to avoid having any conflict that they may come to a fast agreement. But their superficial decisions don't hold up. Generally, fused couples don't make good decisions because they never give the salesperson enough information. To prevent this, the sales professional should ask questions and do more probing.

When a couple is in a power struggle, winning the argument is more important than making a mutually satisfactory purchase. Power strugglers also make poor decisions; it is more important for each party to get his or her way or to be right. To adapt to a power struggle, the sales professional will have to slow down the pace and be prepared to be very patient. You must search for a way to create a win-win solution and find the middle ground. This can be very frustrating when one partner wants all or nothing, an attitude that can kill any deal, anytime.

Donald Meichenbaum, Ph.D., a Canadian psychologist who specializes in cognitive restructuring, says, "You can always find a way to reframe something into a positive without being phony." The technique of "reframing" is a counseling—and communication—tool that helps put a concept in a different light and keep any conversation on solid footing.

For instance, in this chapter's opening example, Mary counterattacks Ralph's disinterested choice of dark orange carpet by saying, "I can't believe you would choose that color." The sales professional might reframe this comment by saying, "Mary, you have very strong feelings about that choice of color. What color do you think would work better?" Reframing doesn't take sides, it just states the information a bit differently in order to get a confirmation or clarification.

As the last resort in a power struggle, a sales professional might have to align himself with the stronger person—the one who is obviously going to get his or her way. Unfortunately, trying to make both people happy in a power struggle usually results in the salesperson's coming out the loser.

In the interdependent stage, each member of the couple might have a totally different idea about what kind of boat or building they want to buy. Yet, via their differences, they continue to gather more data and search for a third solution that will be better than either of their individual ideas. They are able to unify, despite separate opinions, and put forth a joint effort. When they do encounter a hurdle or impasse, all they need from a sales professional is a little space and time to communicate with each other. Pressuring them is the wrong tactic.

Sometimes there is an unspoken decision-maker in the couple's buying situation, whether the couple knows it or not. Even an experienced sales professional can fall victim. Stan was a top-producing Cadillac salesman for more than fifteen years. He had sold to a particular couple in the past and thought he knew them from that previous interaction. One day this couple came into his dealership wanting to purchase a new car. The man was more aggressive during the discussion, and Stan got busy addressing his concerns. Since the man had mentioned that he had diabetes, Stan automatically focused on this important health limitation during his sales presentation. He encouraged the pair to look at vehicles that had more leg room so there would be more ease getting in and out of the car. Meanwhile, the woman seemed uninterested.

Despite bending over backward for this guy, Stan nearly lost the sale. Why? Stan made a giant assumption and a wrong one— the car wasn't for the man at all, but for the woman. He finally picked up enough clues from their conversation that the woman was the prospective car owner and decision-maker in this instance, *but she had not yet participated in the interaction.* Stan's sale was in jeopardy until he realized his error and made attempts to bring the woman back into the conversation in a gentle but probing way—getting her feedback on various aspects and asking how she liked certain features. After bringing her concerns into the discussion, he was able to get the sale back on track. Now Stan advises, "Never assume anything."

Susan Brooks, co-owner with her husband, Barry, of the mail-order business Cookies From Home, uses a specific approach when she calls on a couple who own a business together. She attempts to determine, after a few minutes of conversation, where their strengths and concerns lie. In one couple she was selling to, the man was bottom-line oriented, value conscious, and interested in the return on investment. The woman's major areas of concern were image, presentation, and design. Susan danced between the two people, including them both, but focused on each person's specific style and needs as she spoke to each of them. She steadfastly guards against playing each one against the other in any way. This adaptation technique works well for her and holds promise for others.

Sally Lassen-Krzykos is a financial consultant with Arizona Associates of BMA and is former president of the Phoenix Association of Life Underwriters. She points out that addressing money issues with a couple can elicit very strong emotions—ones that don't usually surface with other concerns, including child-rearing and even religion. In general, if one spouse works and the other spouse doesn't, it's the working spouse who has the final financial say. But if both people are income earners, then they both usually want to be equals in such decisions.

"Never play one against the other," says Lassen-Krzykos. "Some people would advise playing to the person making the decision, but I have better success backing off and listening to both. I turn into a counselor rather than a consultant. You don't want to get in the middle of anything, but if you don't help them down the path, then nothing gets accomplished."

Tips for Men Selling to Couples

What do male salespeople need to do differently when selling to couples? Here are some tips:

Women Want to Be Taken Seriously

Jonathan Thomas Anderson, the top sales professional at one of the Southwest's premier auto dealers, has enjoyed extraordinary success in selling to couples. "The initial contact is very important," he says. "As I greet a couple, I always greet the woman first. She's the primary partner who will eventually say yes or no to any sale, in my opinion."

He continues: "I involve her in all information and fact-finding. Once I start to show the vehicle, I lift the hood—even if she doesn't know anything about an engine—and I explain the features, benefits, and values that the engine can produce. All that's important is that the customer understand why the car's features will benefit her.

"During a test-drive, I always offer keys to the woman first," Anderson goes on. "Even if the man takes the keys, I stop halfway through the test-drive so the woman can also drive. If she doesn't want to, it's because she's afraid. Maybe there's too much traffic or it's a busy intersection. That's fairly normal. If she doesn't take the test-drive at that point, I will go to a more secluded place, stop again, and say, 'Okay, let's go.' On the second try, 99.9 percent of the women will drive it. I say that it's 'the feel of the wheel that makes the deal'—and women make the deal. The man has the ego trip, but the woman still makes the deal.

"When we get back to the dealership, I basically ask the woman point-blank if she likes the vehicle enough to want it while asking the man what he thinks. If she says no, I'm on the wrong vehicle. If it's yes, I share prices and payments."

Accept That Women Are Higher Maintenance Than Men as Customers

You will never offend a couple if you greet the woman first, treat her as a partner in the purchase, and keep her involved throughout the sales process. This needs to be done with eye contact as well as with words. Be very careful to use equal gender terminology, too.

Avoid Patronizing and Condescending

A salesman who treats a woman equally throughout a sale in terms of eye contact, body language, and spoken words can still leave her with a negative impression by calling her dear, honey, or sweetheart at any point. Use her name or "Ms." if you are uncertain. If you must err, err on the side of formality.

Use Active Listening Skills

An effective technique in selling to the "power struggle" couple is active listening. Frequent feedback is what active listening is all about; use it primarily when feelings are strong and a customer's need to be heard is apparent. It's a check for accuracy: Is my impression correct and acceptable to the person who just expressed himself or herself to me?

There are a number of ways that active listening can be used. By paraphrasing the salesperson restates in his or her own words the statement that the customer made. The salesperson acknowledges the apparent feelings expressed in the customer's communication. The goal is to convey understanding and interest in the customer's experience.

An example might go something like this:

MARY: But, I had my heart set on the blue-and-white interior.
SALESPERSON: The blue-and-white interior is very important to you.
JIM: Wait a minute. That price is just way out of line for us.
SALESPERSON: The price isn't acceptable for your current financial setup.

This "mirror" effect is almost a direct paraphrase, but it is effective. Active listening is a communication technique that is well worth studying both for those beginning their career in sales and for the advanced sales professional. The purpose is to develop and convey an accurate understanding of another person's communication. Using it with a couple can help diffuse their feeling that you're biased toward one of them. Requesting feedback keeps the lines of communication open between the couple and the sales professional.

Tips for Women Selling to Couples

Women have different challenges when dealing with couples. They must adapt to the man, of course, but may also find an unexpected challenge with the woman. Here are some perennial basics:

Build Quick Credibility

When credibility must be built instantly, third-party testimonials can be a great tool, so be sure to have some readily available. You can do this by calling satisfied customers and asking them for testimonial letters. For example, you can say, "Sally and Stan, as you know, my business is built by word of mouth, and I feel that having a letter from you would be a tremendous asset to my promotional package. Would you be willing to write me a letter of recommendation?" Save all such letters in a quality-bound notebook and use them as part of your promotional package. You can also build credibility with details such as the plaques on your wall and the photos on your desk.

Decrease Emotional Intensity

Just as it is particularly important that a female sales professional remember to decrease emotional intensity (when she is selling to a man alone), it is also crucial that she take the emotional pulse of both partners into account at the same time. This can be accomplished easily by asking open-ended questions that begin with the emotional timber of the least emotional partner and then slowly raising the emotional intensity.

When emotions appear to be heating up between a couple, the female sales professional should try to become the "neutralizer" and attempt to decrease the emotions between them. Listening to one partner, taking notes, verbally repeating what you heard, and then asking the other partner for his or her thoughts while still taking notes is an excellent way of keeping everyone's emotions under control. After you have neutralized the emotions with an analytical approach, you can then slowly raise the emotional intensity to an appropriate level.

Treat Partners with Equal Respect

One of the most effective ways to create the impression of treating partners with equal respect is to be aware of their body language, tone of voice, rate of speech, and eye contact. This attention to detail helps communicate your equal respect for both partners. Your subtle and unspoken communication signals can often say the most—especially in the case of a female sales professional who may need to build her credibility because of many men's tendency to be condescending.

Pamela Boynton, vice president of marketing for a large office liquidation firm, is well aware of certain techniques that work for selling face-to-face to a couple. She says that when a couple comes through the double doors and she walks up to greet them, she stands in the middle. She makes eye contact with the woman first, to avoid the misconception that Pam is showing preferential treatment toward the man. She always tries to address each party equally and never turns her back on one or the other.

Adapt to the Situation

While the gender issue continues to evolve, women need to learn to adapt to situations with finesse and grace. Don't assume the worst if the male or female partner in a couple doesn't feel comfortable with you. Learning to roll with the punches and using a sense of humor will give you a staying power in your chosen profession.

Sally Lassen-Krzykos described one situation early in her career where she discovered that wives felt threatened by her. She had made an appointment to call on a couple. When she arrived at the door, the wife said, "We have an appointment with the financial consultant."

Sally replied, "I *am* the financial consultant."

The woman responded, "I thought you would be a man. I don't allow my husband to meet with other women in business."

Sally quickly said, "I'm sorry there was a miscommunication. I have several couples with whom I work and have several referral letters I could give you to look over."

The woman said, "I want a *male* consultant." Sally returned to the office, gave the lead to a male consultant, and they split the commission. Sometimes you have to adapt to the situation, even in the extreme.

The Bottom Line on Couples

Mark Tewart, a trainer and coach of salespeople in the auto industry and proprietor of Tewart Enterprises in Shawnee, Kansas, says: "Early in my career in auto sales, I learned a valuable lesson about power struggles between couples. I had been working with a couple for several hours and had helped them select and also test-drive the vehicle they wanted. The couple appeared to be excited and ready to conclude the transaction.

"After coming inside to give them a price estimate, I asked them a closing question to buy the vehicle. The husband turned to the wife and said, 'Honey, what do you think?' The wife looked at her husband and said, 'I don't know. What do *you* think?' The couple repeated the question over and over. Finally, the man said, 'We need to talk about it, so I guess we'll get back to you.'

"Everything had been positive up until the decision time, and both of them had expressed interest in buying the vehicle. After they left, I mentally reviewed the scenario again and again, trying to find my mistake. I came to the conclusion that both parties wanted the vehicle but had a power conflict about making the decision. Neither one wanted to stick his or her neck out and say definitely, 'Yes, I want the vehicle. I think we should get it.'

"In future transactions whenever I heard the question, 'Honey, what do you think?' I realized the man was ready to buy. Now when that time comes, I immediately take control and assume the sale by saying, 'Folks, I *know* you're both going to enjoy this vehicle. How are you going to handle the balance, cash or finance?' Almost every time in my career since that first couple, I've been successful in closing after hearing that magic question—simply by assuming the sale and letting each member of the couple off the hook."

The bottom line is that to "avoid the gopher holes" in selling to couples, you need good communication tools. Learning these Gendersell techniques can help minimize the risk of potentially explosive situations. No single technique works in every case or in every situation, but together they represent some powerful ammunition for maximizing success in the complex field of selling to couples.

Epilogue: Gendersell Success

Adaptation in sales communication means that the sales professional is delivering the message in a way that will be well received by the listener or customer. In his book *Ethics in Human Communication,* Richard Johannesen discusses two extremes in human communication: saying only what the audience wants to hear and conveying a complete lack of understanding or concern for the audience. He says, "The search is for an appropriate point between too much adaptation to the audience and not enough." The Gendersell approach is an ethical adaptation. It allows you to capitalize on customers' liking for people who speak their language without taking advantage of them.

Robert is a good example of a sales professional who applied Gendersell techniques in small ways with big results. He sells accounting services to small- and medium-size businesses, and due to the rapid growth of female-owned companies, he is concentrating on women as potential clients. In the first conversation (whether or not he was the one who initiated the call) Robert suggests, "Tell me more about you." This is obviously a very open-ended comment that can lead to a variety of responses. When the potential purchaser starts talking, Robert learns exactly what is currently important to her and about her: her cash flow, her children, her golf game, her vacation plans, or her company's image.

Robert takes careful, detailed notes and prepares for the next contact. He always starts the telephone conversation by asking, "Is this a convenient time for you to talk briefly?" Following an affirmative response, Robert uses his notes to ask the connecting question or make the appropriate comment: "I noticed the weather in Florida was spectacular last week. That must've been a real plus for your golf game. How often did you play?" Or "I read that there have been some moves in upper management at your company. What's your opinion about the changes?"

By remembering and bringing up details about the client's life, asking opinions instead of telling, and being tuned in to women's business issues and interests, Robert has increased his success in selling to women. Although he thought he was already fairly good at relationship-building skills, with some very specific planned changes in communication he moved from good to superior—and has the results to show for it.

Robert's attempts to woo his female customers isn't a ploy. He really is interested in them, but previously he hadn't communicated that interest in a way they could relate to. Before, he hadn't seemed to take his female customers seriously. Now he does. It works. He's happy. They're happy.

The same point applies to women in sales. Sometimes when we encourage women who work primarily with men to learn more about sports, they respond that they'd feel uncomfortable faking enthusiasm for a topic if they didn't really care. But when examined another way, the saleswoman isn't pretending to like sports, she is instead expressing interest in her customer's interest. Is that being phony?

Bev is a good example of a woman who has dramatically improved her sales to men using the Gendersell approach. By her own admission, Bev's view of gender in the workplace was perhaps more "southern" than those of her peers. She only knew one way to deal with men: to be sweet and slightly coquettish or be simply attentive. This approach doesn't work when you're trying to sell thousands of dollars of consulting services to mainly male decision-makers.

Bev started with reprogramming, although she credits her use of humor as the single most effective change she has made working with men. Once reluctant to call men, she now aggressively makes the initial contact. She has come to enjoy working with men almost more than working with women. She likes their directness, the speed with which they move the business, and the ease with which they respond with humor to her humor.

One technique she used to achieve this was changing her internal monologue about selling to men. Although she was very uncomfortable in the past, she had experienced some success. She focused on those outcomes, reminding herself, "I already have a start, and I can build a history of greater success selling to men." Next, she worked on gaining greater control over what she could control—herself—and worrying less about what she couldn't control—the male customers. She talked more to male friends, colleagues, and relatives about their roles as customers, talked to other sales professionals about selling to men, read more, wrote more, and literally immersed herself in the topic as a way of desensitizing herself.

With this information in hand, Bev became more confident and was then able to take calculated risks. She accomplished this by creating a detailed script for all calls she made to men, from the initial cold call to the close. The script guided her through the rocky waters, although of course it wasn't used as a rigidly read directive. It included a few possible injections of humor, a potential sports reference, and the information she was asking or conveying. By writing the script, Bev removed 70 percent of the anxiety. When she felt in control of herself, she felt more in control of the situation. Less was left to chance.

Bev's biggest sale started with a cold call to a man at one of the largest investment firms in the country. She started in a confident tone with her scripted approach: "Hello, Mr. Ives. I'm calling from the office of Carolyn Warner in Phoenix, Arizona. I see that your company exhibited at the Texas Association of School Administrators Conference last month in Dallas. Carolyn Warner was the closing keynote speaker at the convention. We are sorry we didn't get a chance to talk to you at that time. We thought you might appreciate our introducing our firm to you, as we specialize in connecting private sector companies to key decision-makers within the education community. What methods other than exhibiting at trade shows do you traditionally use to market to education?"

The customer was interested. A second call to assess needs revealed the firm's interest in a greater market share in Arizona, where Bev's firm, Corporate Education // Consulting, Inc., was based. Bev organized a meeting with all the principals of the investment company—an all-male group. When the breakfast meeting started, the owner of CECI talked about the impressive national connections that CECI had with the education industry. Bev noticed the men from the investment firm looked uncomfortable. She gently interrupted the owner of her company, directed her comments to the men, and brought the focus back to CECI's ability to fulfill the needs of the investment firm within the local environment. She knew the local contacts were their immediate concern. Bev closed the sale a week later—the biggest contract CECI had signed to date. It was also Bev's biggest success selling to men.

Marketing, PR, and Advertising

In small business, women and men work in different ways to increase their sales with the opposite sex. Many business leaders are creatively applying the Gendersell principles we espouse.

A somewhat unique application of the Gendersell approach was implemented by small-business owner Anna Marie Prassa and her companies Executive Stress Busters, Inc., and Bio-Therapeutics. Extremely successful in her business, Anna had worked primarily with women. She commented that she was suddenly hit with the realization that "men have a face. Men have a body. They care about appearance and stress reduction and skin care. They're a whole new target market for my company's products and services." Anna realized that selling to these men would not be the same as selling to women. Yes, they cared about some of the same factors, but they couldn't be sold in the same way.

KTGE was a local radio station that used all male announcers and talk show hosts, and appealed primarily to a male market. It also owned an affiliated all-sports station. A perfect context. A great fit. Anna proposed a deal to the station: She'd provide free skin and bio-therapeutic services to men of different ages at the stations and then use them for testimonials when she ultimately bought airtime.

Anna decided on a bold macho approach with some humor, such as: "Only a tough guy can take the sting of a really powerful facial skin treatment. And only a really sexy guy knows how to have great-looking, great-feeling skin—all over!" Bold graphics, big print, and pictures of athletes would be used to defeminize Anna's skin and body care products and services. In some ads a woman extolled the virtues of her man having great healthy skin. In others, athletes connect bio-therapeutics with their general fitness. Another approach tied skin care in with the new men's movement. It's too soon to know if Anna's approach will work, but in all likelihood it will succeed.

In a parallel situation, Elizabeth Arden Salons owner David Stoup is planning to increase the introduction of traditionally female products to a male market. Elizabeth Arden offers a full range of hair, skin, nail, and massage services. Currently, 5 percent of its clients are men. David proposes to increase the proportion to 30 percent. Will his company have to sell, market, and advertise differently in order to accomplish his goal? Absolutely.

David advocates an educational rather than a sales approach with men. He speculates that with this technique men will eventually have as great a need for regular skin care as women do. Other catalysts include the economic pressures of having to look the part in a high-level job and the psychological boost that comes with looking your best.

How About You?

Now it's time for you as a sales professional to put your plan into action. You recognize male-female differences, you understand Gendersell, and you're ready to go. Maybe you'll take an active listening class or a reprogramming seminar. Maybe you'll decide to team up with someone of the opposite sex and trade tips about selling to each other's gender. Perhaps you'll risk approaching a high-level salesperson of the opposite sex to arrange for some mentoring. Or you'll buy season tickets to the Women's National Basketball Association games in your city and take male and female clients as your guests. Being up on movies, sports, books, business, and local events of interest to either sex increases the likelihood of speaking your client's language.

If you haven't made a plan yet, start thinking now about how you're going to influence your customers of the opposite sex more effectively.

Are you ready to develop a more flexible, creative approach to selling?

Have you acknowledged that gender is an enormous differentiating factor between customers?

Are you excited about trying different approaches for men and women?

Have you determined exactly what male-female communication differences you've observed?

Are you ready to try some Gendersell techniques and evaluate the outcome?

Review the techniques and choose three different ones to use within the next month. Write them down in your time management book, scrawl them on Post-its, or tattoo them on your knee, but make sure you do something different—starting now. If you don't expand your skills to keep pace with the changing market, you'll quickly find yourself out of the game. But if you use the Gendersell techniques that will work for you, you'll dramatically increase your sales to the opposite sex and be poised to face a challenging and exciting future.

Bibliography

About Women and Marketing 8: 6 (May 1995).

About Women and Marketing 9: 5 (May 1996).

About Women and Marketing 9: 6 (June 1996).

About Women and Marketing 9: 2 (February 1996).

Alessandra, T., Ph.D., and P. Wexler. *Non-Manipulative Selling* (audiotape). Chicago: Nightingale-Conant, 1985.

Alreck, P. "Commentary: A New Formula for Gendering Products and Brands." *Journal of Product and Brand Management* 3: 1, 6–18.

Anonymous. "Gender Differences and Computer Buying Patterns." *Dealerscope—Merchandising* 37: 5 (May 1995), 47.

Arnott, N. "It's a Woman's World." *Sales and Marketing Management* 147 (March 1995), 54–59.

Barry, D. *Dave Barry's Complete Guide to Guys.* New York: Fawcett Columbine, 1995.

Begley, S. "Gray Matters." *Newsweek.* March 27, 1995, pp. 48–54.

Buskirk, R., and B. Miles. *Beating Men at Their Own Game.* New York: John Wiley and Sons, 1980.

Cartwright, D., and A. Zander, eds. *Group Dynamics, Research and Theory.* New York: Harper and Row, 1953.

Costa, J., ed. *Gender Issues and Consumer Behavior.* Thousand Oaks, CA: Sage Publications, 1994.

Covey, S. *The 7 Habits of Highly Effective People.* New York: Fireside, 1990.

Crispell, D. "Mr. Mom Goes Mainstream." *American Demographics* 16 (March 1994), 59.

Darley, W., and R. Smith. "Gender Differences in Information Processing Strategies: An Empirical Test of the Selectivity Model in Advertising Response." *Journal of Advertising* 24: 1 (Spring 1995), 41–56.

Dholokia, R., B. Pedersen, and N. Hikmet. "Married Males and Shopping: Are They Sleeping Partners?" *International Journal of Retail and*

Distribution Management 23: 3 (1995), 27–33.

Dortch, S. "What's Good for the Goose May Gag the Gander." *American Demographics* 16: 5 (May 1994), 5–6.

Duncan, B., and D. Moynihan. "Applying Outcome Research: Intentional Utilization of the Client's Frame of Reference." *Psychotherapy* 31: 2 (Summer 1994), 294–97.

Farrant, A. "Saleswoman Sales Skills." *American Salesman* 35: 10 (October 1990), 9–12.

Gitomer, J. "Sales Skills for Sales Experts." *Professional Speaker.* May 1996, pp. 10–12.

Glaser, C., and B. S. Smalley. *Swim with the Dolphins.* New York: Warner Books, 1995.

Goff, B., D. Bellenger, and C. Stojack. "Cues to Consumer Susceptibility to Salesperson Influence: Implications for Adaptive Retail Selling," *Journal of Personal Selling and Sales Management* 14: 2 (Spring 1994), 25–39.

Gordon, Thomas. *Leader Effectiveness Training.* Ridgefield, CT: Wyden Books, 1987.

Hall, E. "Desperately Tweeking Susan," *Marketing Week.* February 1, 1994, pp. 55–56.

Hwang, S. "From Choices to Checkout," *Wall Street Journal,* eastern ed. March 22, l994, p. B1+.

Jacques, E. B. "Man to Woman Selling, Do's and Don'ts for Success." *Jeweler's Circular Keystone.* August 1993, part 2, pp. 49–52.

Johannesen, R. L. *Ethics in Human Communication.* Prospect Heights, IL:Waveland Press, Inc., 1990.

Konopacki, A. "Successfully Selling to Most Women." *Agri-Marketing* 33 (October 1995), 60.

Leeming, J. and C. Tripp, eds. Marketing to Women, 1994 and 1995 Compendium of Trends. Boston: About Women, Inc.

Liston, R. "Product Training That Works." *Training.* September 1996, pp. 62–70.

Mellan, O. "Caveat Gender". *Dow Jones Investment Advisor.* June 1996, pp. 89–93.

Miles, R. "The Age of Innovation." Presentation given at the California Psychological Association Convention, April 4, 1997.

Moir, A., and D. Jessel. *Brain Sex.* New York: Carol Publishing Group, 1991.

Myers, G. "Selling (a Man's World)." *American Demographics.* April 1996, pp. 36–42.

Myers, G. *Targeting the New Professional Woman.* Chicago: Probus, 1994.

Bibliography

Popcorn, F., and L. Marigold. *Clicking.* New York: HarperCollins, 1996.

SELL!NG, March 1997, New York: Institutional Investor, Inc.

"The Schmooze Factor," *SELL!NG.* July/August 1996, p. 13.

Schupak, H. T. "New Customers, New Realities." *Jeweler's Circular Keystone.* August 1993, Part 2, p. 6.

————."Meet the Future and It's Female." *Jeweler's Circular Keystone.* August 1993, Part 2, pp. 16–18.

Simons, G., C. Vasquez, and P. Harris. *Transcultural Leadership.* Houston, TX: Gulf Publishing Co., 1993.

Teather, D. "Hidden Gender." *Marketing.* November 30, 1995, pp. 18–19.

Tingley, J. *Genderflex: Men and Women Speaking Each Other's Language at Work.* New York: AMACOM, 1994.

"Trends, Firsts and New Products," December 1995, Boston: About Women, Inc., p. 3.

Trompenaars, F. *Riding the Waves of Culture.* London: The Economist Books, 1993.

Wares, B. Letter to the Editor on the subject of customer service. *SELL!NG* June 1996, p. 9.

Zimbardo, P. G., and M. Leippe. *The Psychology of Attitude Change and Social Influence.* New York: McGraw-Hill, 1991.

For further information on speeches, seminars, consulting, and educational materials, you may contact the authors at:

Lee E. Robert
Cavett Robert Communications
CECI-2701 E. Camelback Road, #295
Phoenix, AZ 85016
(800) 336-8668/Fax: (602) 957-7587
SPEAKERLEE@aol.com
www.Cavett-Robert.com

Judith C. Tingley, Ph.D.
Peformance Improvement Pros, Inc.
1701 N. Central, #10
Phoenix, AZ 85020
(800) 795-4346/Fax: (602) 371-3432
jtingley@gendersell.com
www.gendersell.com

Index

quantitative skills, 88–90, 95, 98,
107–8, 114
questions, 28–29, 39–40, 41–42, 45,
46–47, 51, 56, 68, 93–94, 100,
157, 162
in closing, 139, 140–41, 143
in needs assessment, 40, 103,
113–14, 115
response to, 109–11, 129

random probing, 113
rapport building, 53–54, 70–84, 87, 91,
103–6, 138
cold approaches to, 72–75
pace of, 78–79, 83, 84, 103, 114, 143
warm approaches to, 72, 76–77
real estate sales, 102, 105, 107, 129
recommendations, 141–42, 157–58
reflecting the feeling, 44–46, 94, 114,
150
reframing, 151–52
rehearsal, 69, 125–26
rejection, fear of, 134–35, 136, 143
relationship-building, 19, 27, 28,
38–41, 46, 51–52, 76, 80, 135, 143
female emphasis on, 27, 28, 38,
89–91, 103, 142
learning about, 93–94, 97, 100,
162–63
relationships, professional, male-
female, 11, 59–60, 85–86, 104–5
reprogramming, 64–66, 69, 81–82,
107–8, 136, 162–63
respect, 36–38, 130, 132, 157–58
restating, 44–46
risk taking, 66–67, 72, 92, 106,
134–38, 143

safety, women's concerns about, 106
sales buddy system, 107–8, 166
sales literature, 109–10
sales mode, transition into, 71, 83
Sales Preference Survey, 9, 21, 53
sales professionals:
flexibility needed by, 22–23, 37–38,
69, 77–78, 92–93, 117–18, 135,
145, 158–59
training of, 9, 107–8
women as, 53–54, 68–69, 81, 84

satisfied customers, 141–42, 157
schmoozing, 71–72, 94, 127
scripts, use of, 163
selection interview, 103–4
self-deprecation, 124, 128
self-promotion, 57, 97–98
sensitivity, 80, 124, 134–36
sexual attraction, 71, 81, 109, 135, 138,
143
shopping, 10, 15–18, 22
similarity, 7, 29, 30–31, 74, 83, 87, 99,
100, 103, 149
slickness, 91, 120, 128, 132
small businesses, 164–65
socialization, female, 24–25, 64–66,
81, 97–98
speaking style, gendered, 10, 27–28,
61–64
specificity, 60–61, 109–11, 125–26,
131, 139–40
sports, 18, 162, 165
sports terminology, 17, 58–59, 98–99,
100, 115, 119, 125
stages of communication, 149–53
standing, in presentations, 127
stereotypes, gender, 8, 15, 18–19, 24,
97–98, 119, 122
stress, 62, 65, 123–24, 146
success, defining, 100
suggestions, 50–51, 57, 129, 132, 134

telling, 46–48, 93–94, 113–14, 115,
129, 140–41
test-drive, 154
testimonials, 156–57, 165
thank-you note, 142
training, 107–8
trends, 13–14, 18, 34, 78, 102–3, 111,
117–18, 134
trust-building techniques, 128–29

understanding, 36–38, 48–50, 92, 102,
113, 128, 154, 162

visual aids, 58–59, 124, 129–30, 132,
157

"why" question, 113–14, 115
win-win situations, 61–62, 136–37, 151